TRUE TALES OF ANIMAL HEROES

ALLAN ZULLO

 Troll

To good friends
Ron and Linda Bicksler

CONTENTS

HEROES DON'T HAVE TO BE HUMAN

You can find heroes in classrooms and sports arenas, in police uniforms and surgical scrubs, in newspapers and history books.

You can also find heroes in the animal world.

Some people claim that animals can't show compassion and courage like humans can. The evidence is overwhelming, however, that animals are capable of acting with kindness and concern toward humans—especially those who desperately need help.

For instance, a Border collie and a Rottweiler teamed up to rescue a drowning boy. A devoted cat fought off an intruder who was assaulting a young girl.

You might expect a loyal pet dog or cat to come to the aid of its master, but even animals in the wild have performed astounding, kindhearted deeds. Two elk saved a lost boy from freezing to death. A pod of dolphins foiled a shark attack on a helpless swimmer.

Yes, heroes come in all shapes and sizes. They gallop and swim and fly. They snort and whinny and bark—and they often come to the rescue at the critical moment when a victim has lost all hope of getting help.

In this book, you'll read remarkable stories of animals whose spirit and bravery saved the lives of young people in gripping life-or-death ordeals. Although the heroic incidents are true, the dialogue and situations have been dramatized and certain names and events have been changed.

If trouble strikes, who ya gonna call? How about Sparky the cat, Rita the parrot, or Smurf the horse.

THE NIGHT VISITORS

I'm going to die. Nobody's coming for me. Nobody even knows I'm here.

Bryan Palmer wanted to cry, but the fourteen-year-old was too exhausted and cold. His body shivered uncontrollably from the wind-whipped, bone-numbing snow. He crouched in the darkness under an evergreen, wondering if this unexpected September storm would ever end—and, more important, if he would make it through the night.

I'm so tired. I just want to go to sleep. . . . No, I can't. If I do, I'll freeze to death. I have to stay awake. Keep rubbing those arms. Why didn't I listen to Dad and bring a heavier jacket? What an idiot I am. This could be my last night on earth.

Maybe just a little catnap. My eyelids are so heavy. . . . No! If I'm asleep, I'll be easy pickings for animals. What a tasty meal I'd make for a bear or a pack of wolves.

Hey, something's out there. I hear snorting. What is it? It's coming closer. . . .

Earlier that day, Bryan, his dad, Carl, Uncle Lenny, and Bryan's cousin Steve had set up a base camp in the High Uintas Primitive Area in the northeast corner of Utah. It was the beginning of their fourth annual three-day hunting trip. Their prey was the ruffed grouse, a chicken-shaped game bird that is part of the pheasant family.

Like his father, Bryan loved to hunt, but not for the pleasure of the kill. He shot only those animals he could eat. A careful hunter who had taken several gun safety courses, Bryan was an excellent marksman.

His packing skills, however, were those of a mere beginner. He always packed too light, never bringing enough snacks for himself or the proper clothing because he didn't want to lug the gear. No matter how many times his father warned him about the ever-changing mountain weather, Bryan always left his warm clothes at home.

The first day of their hunting trip was cool, with cottonlike clouds floating among the mountain peaks. Clad in ammunition belts and orange vests, the four-some cradled their empty shotguns and journeyed out from their base camp.

"Shouldn't you bring a sweatshirt?" Carl asked his son. "The weather can change quickly."

Bryan, wearing jeans and a T-shirt under a light jacket, waved his hand. "Don't worry about it, Dad."

"At least take your rain gear."

"I feel like a packhorse now. I'll be fine with my jacket."

Carl shook his head. "Don't complain to me when you get wet. You're not getting my rain gear."

"I don't want it. Come on, Dad, give me a break. I'm fourteen and—"

"I know. You're old enough to make your own decisions." Under his breath, Carl added, "I just wish you'd make more of the right ones."

During their trek to a new hunting area, Uncle Lenny asked the two boys, "Have you ever been approached by a grouse who was happy to see you?"

"Huh?" said Bryan, his eyebrows raised.

Lenny chuckled and explained, "I know a friend who was walking along an old logging road, minding his own business, when a grouse came out in the open, clucking to beat the band. These dumb birds have actually followed people through the woods."

"Really?"

"Scout's honor. The problem is, the grouse get confused about the difference between being nice and being mean. They'll walk behind you one minute and nip at your ankles the next. Weird birds."

"But tasty ones," Bryan reminded him.

They soon arrived at a clearing where the summer wildflowers competed with the color-changing leaves of fall. As the hunters spread out, Bryan heard a grouse calling in the woods beside a path. "Dad, I'm going up on that ridge," he announced.

"Don't stray too far," Carl warned. "We've never hunted in this area before."

"I'll be fine. I'll stick to the path."

Carl told the others, "If we get separated, meet back here at this meadow no later than four o'clock."

About two hundred yards (182 m) into a forest of spruce and pine, Bryan heard a sharp "quit-quit"—the distinctive call of an alarmed ruffed grouse. Bryan loaded his weapon. *Keep making that noise, birdie. Or better yet, why don't you come out and greet me?* Tracking the call, the teen walked off the path and peered through the trees but couldn't spot the bird. *Just like Uncle Lenny says, "A motionless grouse is an invisible grouse."*

Suddenly, the bird exploded skyward in a thunderous flapping of wings. Caught off guard, Bryan fired instinctively but missed. *How can a bird that big fly that fast through all those trees?* he wondered as he lowered his shotgun.

Realizing he was off the trail and walking deeper into the woods, Bryan began snapping twigs and placing rocks on top of logs as markers to guide him back to the path.

About an hour later, he emerged from the evergreen forest into an alpine meadow where Mother Nature presented him with a visual treat.

Across the way stood a handsome bull elk. The animal held his head high as if showing off his magnificent antlers branching out to a spread of five feet (1.5 m).

Bryan raised his shotgun and put the elk in his sights. "Oh, man, would I like to bring you down," Bryan whispered.

The wind suddenly shifted, blowing much cooler air from behind the teen. Catching a whiff of a human's scent, the elk darted back into the cover of the forest.

Bryan looked over his shoulder and saw gray cloud banks rising over the ridge behind him. A bolt of lightning streaked across the darkening sky. "One thousand one, one thousand two . . ." Bryan counted. When he reached five, the thunderclap echoed off a nearby peak.

Bryan knew that five seconds between a flash of lightning and a clap of thunder mean a storm is a mile (1.6 km) away. Thunderstorms in the mountains typically move about a mile (1.6 km) every two or three minutes.

I better get out of here. The metal in my gun could attract lightning. Besides, I'm the tallest object in this meadow. I'll be much safer in the woods. He had just started back when the clouds opened, pelting him with cold rain.

Bryan took the shells out of his gun as a safety precaution as he scurried into the woods. But in his haste, he forgot to look for the markers that would guide him to the path.

I think I came this way. Or was it that way? It doesn't matter. I'll just hide under that big rock outcropping. These mountain storms don't last very long. When it's over, I'll figure out how to get back.

The rain slacked off within ten minutes. However, the temperature had dropped considerably. Bryan checked his watch. It was three-thirty. He tried to retrace his steps but couldn't find any of his markers, and the low-hanging clouds blotted out the sun so he couldn't get a fix on his bearings. He examined the base of several tree trunks until he spotted moss, which tends to grow on the north side. Bryan knew he needed to go south, so he walked in the opposite direction from where the moss was growing. Soon an uneasy feeling grew inside him.

Everything looks the same. I thought I knew my way around here. Man, it's getting cold. I wish I'd brought my sweatshirt.

Bryan walked south for a half hour without hitting the path. *Shoot, I've gone too far,* he realized. *It's four o'clock. I've got to find that path. Dad is going to start to worry.* He headed back in a northwesterly direction. About forty minutes later, he came upon an alpine meadow that looked familiar. *I don't believe it—I'm back where I was when the storm hit!*

"Come on, Bryan, think!" the boy muttered to himself. "Look for your markers." He walked around the meadow, hoping he would recognize where he had first entered. But the fading light made everything look different.

In desperation, Bryan fired two shots into the air, hoping his fellow hunters would hear them. He strained his ears, waiting for a gunshot reply, a shout of recognition, or a whistle. But all he heard was the trees groaning in the blustery wind. He reloaded his shotgun and fired again. *Come on, answer me! Please, someone answer!*

Hearing no response, Bryan plopped down in the tall grass, trying to ignore the sinking feeling in the pit of his stomach. *I'm cold and hungry. I'm over an hour late and totally lost. What more could happen to me?*

The rain began falling again. Only this time it was mixed with ice.

Carl gripped his cellular phone so tightly, he was nearly crushing it.

"Hello, sheriff's office? Look, I need help. My son, Bryan, is missing. He's fourteen. We were hunting on Flat Top Mountain and he strayed from our group. We were supposed to meet back here at Benson's Ridge two hours ago. I think he's lost. We've shouted and fired our guns, but we haven't heard any response. You've got to send a search team up here. If the weather gets any worse, it'll start snowing."

* * *

Bryan had been wandering for nearly three hours. The rain had turned to snow and the sky had grown darker. Adding to his misery, his light jacket wasn't waterproof and did little to ward off the cold.

Bryan couldn't stop shivering—both from fear and from cold. *Keep walking. Don't stop. Got to keep a clear head. Man, this shotgun feels like it weighs a hundred pounds.*

Bryan's top priority had changed from finding his way back to simply surviving through the night. *I sure wish I had brought my warmer jacket. How could I have been so stupid? I've got to start a fire.*

Crouching under a thick evergreen, Bryan collected a few downed branches. He pulled out his pocket knife and whittled away the wet bark. Next he carved the dry wood underneath into paper-thin shavings. He opened a few shells and poured out the gunpowder, then tried to light the kindling with matches he was carrying in his pocket. But the mixture of wet snow and wind made it impossible.

In anger and frustration, Bryan kicked the kindling into the snow. *There's nothing else I can do. Dad's probably called for a rescue team. I better stay in one place.*

Rescue team leader Buck Mathews stood next to his search dog, a golden retriever named Goldie. She was sniffing a piece of Bryan's clothing that Carl had given them.

"We'll see if Goldie can pick up the scent and track him," said Mathews. "Carl, does your son have protective gear?"

"No."

"Then we'll head out right now. If hypothermia sets in, he could be in real danger."

In cold weather, survival depends on conserving one's body heat. Hypothermia begins when the body's temperature falls below normal, triggering uncontrollable shivering. As the body continues to chill, the shivering grows more violent. The muscles stiffen and the mind begins to break down, causing victims to say and do crazy things.

"You've got to find him soon," Carl pleaded. "There's no way Bryan can survive the night on his own."

It was nine o'clock and very dark. The snow continued to pile up.

They're not coming for me tonight, Bryan thought. *Maybe they'll find me in the morning. I just hope I'm still alive when they do . . . if they do.*

Sitting under the branches of the evergreen, Bryan tucked his knees to his chin and rocked back and forth in a futile effort to stay warm. *Don't fall asleep. Fight it. Fight it.*

Bryan's conversation with himself came to an abrupt end when he heard an animal snorting close by. He picked up his shotgun and loaded it. Unable to see in the dark and snow, he slid behind the tree trunk and listened.

It sounds like more than one animal. What are they? Coyotes? Wolves? Grizzlies? Well, whatever they are, they know I'm here. Maybe I can scare them.

Bryan jumped to his feet and roared, "Go away! Get outta here! Scram!" He found a few large stones and hurled them in the direction of the animals. They trotted off but returned a few minutes later. Bryan was poised to shoot, but his finger was too numb from the cold to feel the trigger. He was shaking so badly he wasn't sure he could hit anything anyway.

Bryan crept out from under the branches and peered into the snowy darkness, trying to get a better look at the animals. He lifted his shotgun, then he put it back down. A smile of relief spread across his face.

He could make out two big, gray, four-legged animals about five feet (1.5 m) tall at the shoulder. The shoulders were higher than the hindquarters, giving them a humpbacked appearance. They had short necks and long muzzles. They were female elk.

As the elk fearlessly approached the shivering teen, they lowered their heads, sniffing and studying him. For a brief moment, Bryan forgot he was lost and in danger of freezing to death. He had never seen elk that close before and stared at them in fascination. *They're not afraid of me*, he marveled.

A gust knocked snow off a branch, splattering Bryan's head. By the time he had wiped his face, the elk had gone. He huddled under the tree again, wishing he could stop shaking. He knew shivering was the first sign of hypothermia.

I should have ridden one of those elk out of here. They probably knew the way to Dad. I'm so cold . . . and so tired. Don't fall asleep . . . don't fall . . .

Bryan drifted off to sleep—a sleep which had the potential to kill him. But about five in the morning, he woke up on the hard ground, his muscles stiff. *I dozed off! I can't do that. I could die that way. What if the rescuers walked by when I was asleep? How stupid! Hey, I'm not shivering anymore. I feel warmer. What's that smell? It's like wet fur.*

Bryan sat up and rubbed his eyes. *I'm not dreaming this, am I? No, what I'm seeing is real—real incredible!*

To his utter amazement, both elk lay beside him, one on each side, their backs nearly touching him. *Now I see why I didn't freeze to death during the night. You two kept me warm!*

The breaking dawn revealed at least four inches of snow on the ground, but the storm was over. Seeing the elk and an end to the storm lifted Bryan's spirits. He was so grateful that he wanted to pat the sleeping animals, but he was afraid he'd startle them.

The elk began to stir, making soft, high-pitched grunts. Then they snorted and stood up. Sniffing the air, they quickly trotted off toward the north slope.

"Hey, where are you going?" shouted Bryan. "Come back. Well, thanks for keeping me warm. I couldn't have made it through the night without you."

Suddenly Bryan heard a dog barking. The barking grew louder, accompanied by a human voice coming from the woods on the other side of the meadow.

Bryan's heart leaped for joy. He scrambled to his feet and slogged through the wet snow as fast as he could. Seconds later, he spotted a golden retriever wearing a red SEARCH vest, followed by Buck Mathews.

"Over here! Over here!" Bryan shouted, wildly waving his arms and jumping up and down.

"Are you Bryan Palmer?" yelled the rescuer.

"Yes!"

"Are you all right?"

"I am now!"

Mathews checked the boy for frostbite, but there wasn't any. "Did you find shelter?"

"Not really."

"Exposure in the weather we had last night would kill anyone without shelter within a matter of hours, especially with the light clothes you have on. How did you survive?"

"Two elk saved my life."

As they returned to the command post, Bryan told Mathews the story of his late-night companions.

"Elk are very shy creatures," said Mathews. "They aren't known to approach humans. Bryan, you did suffer from hypothermia, and one of its effects is that you imagine all sorts of things. Those elk really weren't there."

"But it's true, I swear." Yet Bryan was too wet, cold, and tired to turn around and show him the proof.

After Bryan was taken to the hospital for observation, another member of the rescue team, Deputy Stan Sandberg, decided to check out the boy's story. He hiked back to the spot where Bryan had been found and followed the teen's tracks to an evergreen tree.

When Sandberg returned to the sheriff's office, he told Buck Mathews, "I found two sets of fresh elk prints leading away from the evergreen tree where Bryan stayed last night. But I didn't see any hoofprints going to the tree. That means the elk were under the tree during the snowfall. That's not all. I also found depressions in the wet ground fitting the size and shape of two elk. Buck, the kid was telling the truth!"

Meanwhile, at the hospital, Bryan told his father, "I've made an important decision. I don't ever want to go hunting again."

"Because you got lost?"

"No, that's not it. How can I possibly take the life of another wild animal after two wild animals saved my life?"

ATTACK CAT

Micki Flint doesn't believe that black cats bring bad luck. After what her black cat, Shade, did for her, it's easy to understand why.

Shade literally dropped into the life of the brown-haired grade-schooler. Micki lived in the country in a double-wide mobile home with her mother, Tilly, a waitress, and her father, Merle, a long-distance truck driver.

One morning, after her mother had left for work, Micki stood by the bus stop a hundred yards (91 m) from her house. She was chatting with Sam and Jake, two older boys who lived nearby, when a beat-up blue pickup truck weaved down the road.

"What's wrong with that driver?" she asked.

"I don't know, but we better move back from the road," warned Jake.

The three kids scrambled up an embankment as the tire-squealing pickup swayed from lane to lane. When it reached them, the truck screeched to a stop. A heavyset, middle-aged woman, her bright red hair in curlers, leaned out of the driver's side.

"Hey, you!" she shouted at the three startled kids. "Want a cat?"

"Nah," replied Jake, "I'm a dog person."

"Me too," Sam said. "I've already got two dogs."

"What about you, missy?" the woman asked Micki.

"I don't think so. My mama has allergies and—"

"And I've got scratches all over my arms," snapped the woman, sticking out a chubby arm crisscrossed with bloody claw marks. "This mangy furball attacked me while I was driving."

She reached down, muttered a few nasty words, and grabbed a scrawny, squirming black cat by the scruff of his neck. The yowling cat twisted his body and sank his back claws into her wrist.

"Ouch!" she screeched. "Here, little girl, he's yours now!" The woman flung the cat toward Micki. By the time the cat landed on all fours in a patch of weeds, the pickup truck had roared off.

Jake let out a low whistle. "I guess we won't be seeing any 'Be Kind to Animals' bumper stickers on her truck," he said.

Micki kneeled down, but the cat arched his back and hissed at her. "Here, kitty, kitty. It's okay. Don't be afraid."

The cat spat at her and backed away. He tried to run, but his right hind leg was injured. He limped under a nearby rotting log. "He's hurt. We've got to help him," Micki cried.

"The bus is coming," Sam said.

"But I can't just leave him here."

When the bus pulled up, the driver opened the door and the boys climbed on. Micki didn't.

"Are you coming?" the driver asked her.

Micki looked at the frightened, injured cat and then at the bus. *Mama's going to kill me for this*, she thought. "Go ahead. I'm staying."

The bus driver shook her head, closed the door, and stepped on the gas. *Oh, great. What have I done? I'm going to be in so much trouble*. Micki unslung her book bag and crept toward the cat. Reading the fear in his eyes, Micki cooed and talked sweetly to him. "Don't be scared, kitty. I just want to help you. Come here. I won't hurt you."

The cat let out a low moan and backed under the log as far as he could. Micki reached into her book bag and pulled out the ham sandwich she had made for lunch. She tore off a piece of ham and held it out to the cat. He mewed but refused to move. She tossed the ham so that it landed right under his nose. He sniffed the meat and then gobbled it.

"Good kitty!" Micki praised. "Here, have some more. I wonder if you're thirsty too." She took a bottle of water from her book bag and poured some into her cupped palm. Slowly she brought her hand toward the cat. This time, he stretched forward to lick a few drops.

For the next half hour, Micki patiently tried to gain the cat's trust. But every time she attempted to gently pull him out from his hiding place, he hissed at her. Sighing, the girl sat down next to him and opened her science book. "Since I'm not in class today because of you, I better read the next chapter in this book," she told the cat. "Then I won't feel so guilty about missing school."

Two hours passed while Micki read her textbooks. She stopped occasionally, trying to coax the cat out from under the log. But the animal refused to budge.

Her vigil ended when a car stopped and honked. Micki looked up and gulped. "Mama!"

"What are you doing here?" thundered Tilly, leaping out of the car. "You had me worried half to death!"

"I'm sorry. I missed the school bus and—"

"Why didn't you phone me at the restaurant? I got a call from school saying you hadn't shown up. I phoned home but there was no answer. I couldn't imagine what had happened to you!"

"I know. I'm sorry. I just couldn't leave this cat," Micki said, pointing toward the log. "He's hurt and scared. A mean lady threw him out of her truck."

Tilly's frown softened when she spotted the black cat. She walked over to the log and bent down. "Here, kitty, kitty."

Suddenly, the cat let out a yowl and sprang forward into the weeds. He hopped around, hissing and attacking something that neither Micki nor her mother could see. Moments later, he triumphantly limped out and laid a dead snake at Tilly's feet.

"Look, Micki, he's killed a young rattler!"

"That snake would've given you a wicked bite. Can we keep the cat, Mama?"

"I don't think so. Your daddy will pitch a fit, and you know I have allergies."

"But, Mama, the cat just saved your life."

Tilly smiled. "Tell you what. Let's walk home. If he follows us, we'll feed him. But he stays outside. And you'll still have to deal with your daddy when he gets back from his trip. If he says no, the cat goes."

Micki threw her arms around her mother. "Thank you, Mama!" Turning toward the cat, she said, "Follow me, kitty." To her great disappointment, the cat hobbled into the woods.

"Don't go after him," Tilly warned. "You'll only scare him. Get in the car. I've got to take you to school and get back to work before the lunch crowd arrives."

For the next three nights, Micki put a bowl of milk by the back door. Each morning, the milk was gone. There was no sign of the cat—except for a dead mouse placed near the back step each day.

On Saturday afternoon, Micki was helping her mother pin sheets on the clothesline when Tilly pointed to their bird feeder and complained, "Look at that squirrel. He's eating all the seeds." She waved her arms and yelled, "Beat it!"

Swishing its bushy tail, the squirrel continued to munch away as another squirrel bounded toward the feeder. Suddenly, a black flash leaped out of a nearby bush and charged after the squirrel on the ground, who scrambled for the safety of an elm tree. The alarmed squirrel on the feeder jumped off and headed in the opposite direction.

"Mama, look! It's the black cat!" The cat sprawled at the base of the elm tree and gazed smugly at the squirrel chattering angrily above him.

Micki slowly walked over to the cat and knelt down beside him. She was delighted that he didn't run away. As she stroked his back, she said, "Listen, Mama. He's purring. Can we keep him?"

"He'll need to stay outside—and you'll need to get your father's approval."

"I'll feed him and take care of him and love him."

"It sounds like he'll have it made in the shade."

"That's it!" Micki beamed. "That's what I'm going to name him—Shade."

Later that evening, Merle returned from his trip. Micki ran out the door and greeted her father with a warm hug and a big smooch.

"Hi, Princess. Say, that's some welcome. You must want something, right?"

"No, I already have it—that is, if it's okay with you. Please say yes, Daddy."

"What is it?"

"The cutest little cat you ever saw. His name is Shade."

Merle rolled his eyes. "Not a cat. You know I don't like them. And what about your mother's allergies?"

"He'll stay outside. Mama already said it's okay with her."

Right on cue, Shade pranced around the corner of their home with a dead mouse in his mouth. Merle had to smile. "Well, I guess we could use a good mouser around here. He has to be checked out by the vet first. If everything's okay, he can stay—but only outside. Deal?"

"Deal!" Micki squealed, hugging her dad.

Shade was examined by the vet, who guessed the cat was about two years old. "People abandon their pets on the side of the road all the time," the vet said. "Shade is lucky he found you."

But it was Micki who truly was the lucky one. Shade became more than her feline friend. He became her lifesaver.

Shade was an all-star cat. He terrorized the squirrels and rid the yard of field mice and small snakes. He had his own little spot in the crawl space under the Flints' mobile home. Occasionally, when she was home alone, Micki would sneak Shade inside and spoil him with a slice of ham.

One night, Micki was home alone while Tilly worked the night shift at the restaurant and Merle was off on another trip. When a bad thunderstorm struck, the girl brought Shade inside to keep her company.

The cat snuggled in Micki's lap while she watched television. Suddenly, Shade lifted his head. His ears stood at attention.

"What's the matter, Shade?"

The cat jumped off the couch and paced in front of the door. "Shade, it's just a bad storm. We're safe here."

Then a sharp knock at the door startled Micki. She got off the couch and peeked through the curtain. A long-haired man in his twenties stood outside, drenched from the downpour. Micki had never seen him before and knew better than to open the door to a stranger.

She tiptoed back to the couch and hid behind it. The man began pounding on the door. "Hello?" he called out. "I know someone is in there. Your light is on and I can hear the TV. I need your help. I have car problems. My wife and baby are in the car and I need to use your phone. Please. I'm getting soaked out here."

Micki got up from behind the couch and hesitated. She went to the window and tried to get a glimpse of the disabled car, but she couldn't see anything through the rain and darkness. Meanwhile, the man continued to pound on the door. "Please help us."

Meanwhile, Shade, his tail fluffed up from fear, kept slinking back and forth and growling.

I guess it would be all right if I talked to him, Micki told herself. *But I won't let him inside.* After checking that the security chain was latched, she unbolted the front door and cracked it open.

"Oh, thank goodness," the man sighed. "Can I come in and call a tow truck? I want to get my wife and baby home."

Shade crouched at Micki's feet and hissed at the stranger. Then the cat swiped at the screen door that separated him from the man.

"I can't let you come into the house." *Don't tell him you're home alone.* "Um . . . my mom is asleep and I don't want to wake her."

"I understand. Can you call for me? I'll just wait outside here in the rain."

"Sure." Micki closed the door and went into the kitchen, where her parents kept the phone book. She had punched in the first three numbers of a towing service when she heard a loud crack.

Micki whirled around and screamed as the man slammed his shoulder into the front door, which she had failed to rebolt. The door flew open, breaking the security chain. The intruder charged into the kitchen and ripped the phone cord out of the wall.

"Who else is in the house?" he snarled. "Tell me!"

"N—no one. I—I'm all alone."

"Good." The man's dripping, scraggly hair clung to his face, making him appear even more terrifying than he already looked. His murderous eyes darted around the kitchen. "Got anything to eat?"

"There's food in the refrigerator." Micki could barely choke the words out of her mouth.

The intruder brutally shoved her to the floor. "Now stay there and don't move!" He opened the refrigerator and guzzled milk from the carton. Then he grabbed some leftover meatloaf, shoveling it into his mouth with his hands.

Micki cowered in the corner and began to whimper.

"Shut up!" he snapped

"I can't help it. I'm scared!"

After swallowing a chunk of cheese, the man growled, "Are there any men's clothes in this dump?"

She nodded. "In the first bedroom." As he headed to the back of the house, Micki tried to escape through the back door. But the intruder yanked her by the arm and spun her around. Then he slapped her across the face, sending her sprawling against the wall.

As the assailant raised his hand to hit her again, Shade attacked. Baring his sharp claws and teeth, the cat vaulted onto the kitchen table, then leaped onto the man's chest. The feline fury lunged at the intruder's throat and clamped down hard with his fangs.

The man hollered in pain and whirled around the kitchen, punching the ferocious cat. But Shade hung on, clawing and yowling like a banshee. Bleeding from the face and neck, the man stumbled backward, knocking a kitchen chair to the floor. Then he grabbed Shade by the throat and tried to strangle the cat. But Shade squirmed out of the intruder's suffocating grip and slashed at his face with his back claws.

The assailant hurled the cat to the floor and reeled around the kitchen, wiping blood off his face with his torn shirt. Before the man could recover, Shade leaped on him again, clawing and biting.

Screaming in agony, the man slammed Shade against the table, then rushed out the back door. The injured cat tumbled to the floor and lay still.

Micki, sobbing hysterically, crawled over to her dazed cat. "Shade! Shade! You poor thing!" She picked him up and cradled him in her arms. His breathing was heavy and blood trickled from his mouth. She wrapped him in a towel and set him on the couch. Then she ran next door to call 911.

Early the next morning, sheriff's deputies nabbed the attacker, who turned out to be an escapee from a nearby prison. He had stolen a car that had spun out of control and crashed on the wet pavement by the bus stop near Micki's home.

Meanwhile, Micki received treatment for cuts and bruises. Shade was treated at the vet's for a broken rib and a concussion.

When word spread of Shade's heroic deed, friends and strangers came to the house to give him presents—everything from gourmet cat food to toys.

The county humane society even awarded Shade a gold medal for his bravery.

Shade enjoyed all the attention. He let the strangers pet him and photograph him. But he hissed at one heavyset woman in a baseball cap. When Micki apologized, the woman said, "It's okay. Sometimes cats just don't like certain people." The woman opened her purse and handed Micki some money. "Here, put this toward the vet's bills."

Micki counted the money. "Fifty dollars! Awesome! Thank you, ma'am." As the woman walked away, Micki thought, *She looks familiar. I wonder where I've seen her before.* The woman took off her baseball cap, letting her bright red hair fall to her shoulders. Then she hopped behind the wheel and drove off in her beat-up blue pickup truck.

FIRE DOG

Chani Mason and her brother, Kip, gazed into each cage at the animal shelter, hoping to make a heart-to-heart connection with the right dog. It wasn't easy.

They fell for the fox terrier, the bloodhound, the beagle, and the collie.

"This is too hard, Kip," complained fourteen-year-old Chani. "I want to take all of them home. It breaks my heart that they've been abused or abandoned."

"Let's keep looking," said Kip, who was fifteen. "There's got to be one in here that's just right for us."

They bent down in front of another cage and stared at a medium-sized white-and-tan female mutt. The dog stuck her nose through the wire mesh and parted her lips.

"Look, Kip, she's smiling at us."

The dog backed up and sat down as if to give the kids a better look at her. Then she walked in a circle before returning to the front of the cage.

"She *is* smiling, Chani! Cool." Turning to the shelter volunteer, he said, "We'd like to see her, please."

As soon as her cage door opened, the dog charged out, jumped right into Chani's arms, and began licking her face. "Stop! Stop!" Chani giggled.

"What's the background on this dog?" Kip asked the volunteer.

"She's about six months old, a mixed breed— probably terrier and retriever. She was brought in by a couple who couldn't care for her anymore. At least they didn't throw her on the side of the road like so many people do. She's healthy and, as you can see, very loving."

"She certainly gave me a licking," said Chani. "What do you think, Kip?"

"I think we found ourselves a dog."

They had found a dog that would soon be a hero.

The kids named the dog Maxine after their favorite aunt. Maxine proved to be a loyal, loving, obedient family pet. Her personality couldn't get much sunnier. But she did have a strange thing about bells. Whenever she heard the doorbell or a church bell, she would let out a howl of recognition and run in circles. If she was outside and heard the bell from the ice cream truck, Maxine would chase it, unless one of the Masons ordered her to heel. Other than this strange quirk, she was a wonderful dog.

One week a month, Kip and Chani had to fend for themselves in the evenings while their dad and mom—a police officer and a nurse—worked the night shift. Their parents worried that Chani and Kip were such sound sleepers they could snooze through an emergency. There was no guarantee they would hear the smoke detectors or a tornado or a neighbor's cry for help. Chani used two alarm clocks, one on each side of her bed, to rouse her in the morning. Kip woke up to a radio alarm turned full blast to an alternative rock station.

One frigid winter night, Kip and Chani were home alone, watching a video in the living room. They huddled under a blanket on the couch because the faulty furnace wasn't pumping out enough heat. The wind whistled outside, making them feel even colder. An electric space heater and Maxine, who was lying in Chani's lap, helped ward off the chill.

When it was time for bed, Maxine trotted into the utility room and hopped into a large basket by the washer and dryer. She curled up on a plaid comforter that Aunt Maxine had made especially for her.

Before heading upstairs, the kids flipped a coin to see who would get to use the space heater in their room. Kip won. He plugged it in by his bed and dove under the covers. Chani donned her thickest flannel nightie and heavy wool socks. Then she slipped into bed and pulled the blankets tightly around her neck. By midnight, the kids and their dog were deep in dreamland.

"Oh, Kip, you're so handsome. You're the coolest guy in class," Sandra Bowles whispered, smiling as she snuggled closer to him.

"I think you're the most beautiful girl in the entire school. I can't believe you even noticed me."

"Shut up and let's kiss."

Kip gulped as Sandra pinned him against the wall and planted a long kiss on his lips. The kiss was much wetter than he expected. After they broke from their clinch, he was shocked to see Sandra light a cigarette and blow smoke his way.

"Let's kiss again," she purred between puffs.

Kip began coughing as she gave him a smoky smack on the lips.

Gagging, Kip blurted, "Get away! I can't breathe. The smoke is killing me." He tossed his head back and forth on the pillow as he woke up from his dream. His eyes stung and his face felt wet. His lungs ached, and a heavy weight on his chest made it hard to breathe.

Kip realized that Sandra was neither kissing him nor smoking. Instead, Maxine was licking his face, whining in his ear, and pawing his chest.

"Get off me," Kip grumbled. "I can't breathe." After another moment, he became aware that his breathing difficulties had nothing to do with the dog.

Smoke was billowing through his bedroom from crackling flames that were climbing the drapes and the wall.

"Fire!" he yelped, gagging from the smoke. Dazed and confused, Kip rolled out of bed and tumbled to the floor. Unable to see in the smoke, he groped for the door. Maxine, barking madly, hopped off the bed and landed beside Kip. He reached for her collar and said, "Get me out of here, girl."

Together they made it to the open bedroom door and into the pitch-black hallway. Kip stayed on his belly because he knew the remaining air would hover below the suffocating smoke.

"Chani! Chani! Wake up!" The smoke was sinking lower and time was running out. "Maxine, go get Chani!"

The dog barked once, then scurried into Chani's room, where flames had already broken through the wall. The dog jumped on her bed and began licking the girl's face and barking. But Chani rolled over and threw the covers over her head.

Maxine clenched the bedspread in her mouth and pulled it off, causing the sleeping girl to roll up into a ball. The dog then grabbed Chani's foot in her teeth and pulled the girl's leg to the edge of the bed.

Finally, Chani woke up. "Ouch! Hey, stop that!" she protested. She sat up and immediately began gagging from the smoke. Seeing the flames lashing the wall, she screamed and bolted out of bed.

Maxine barked and led her to the hallway, which was now hot and thick with smoke and flames. Shuffling on her knees, Chani held onto Maxine's tail as the dog crawled down the hallway to Kip, who lay prone at the top of the stairs. Together, the teens and their dog scrambled down the steps and out the front door. Kip sprinted next door to call 911. By the time firefighters arrived, flames had engulfed the second floor.

Fortunately, the soot-covered kids and their dog were not injured. When they told the fire captain how Maxine had awakened them, he declared, "Without that dog, you kids would have died from smoke inhalation or severe burns. She saved your lives."

Investigators discovered that a short in the space heater in Kip's room had started the fire. The blaze was so destructive that the entire house had to be remodeled. The family lost most of its possessions. But at least Kip and Chani had their lives—thanks to Maxine.

Because it would be months before they could move back home, the Masons rented a house in a nearby neighborhood. One sunny Saturday afternoon, Maxine was sitting in the front yard of the rented house when two girls passing by on bikes decided to race. "One, two, three, go!" one of the girls yelled. Then she rang the bell on her handlebar.

The bell stirred Maxine's weird quirk, and she barreled after them. None of the Masons saw Maxine take off.

The dog happily tailed the two cyclists for several blocks. When the kids crossed busy Patton Avenue, Maxine did too, although the honking horns and heavy traffic startled her.

Once safely across, she continued to follow the girls to their house, where they got off their bikes and headed inside. Their father, who was not a dog lover, shooed Maxine away. She wasn't used to having anyone yell at her, and she ran off with her tail between her legs.

The dog ambled down a side street and through an alley. Soon she was totally lost. She had never been this far away from home before. The traffic, the kids, and the mean man had thrown off her navigational skills.

As night fell, Maxine tried to pick up a scent, any scent that would lead her back home. Meanwhile, the Masons drove around the neighborhood, searching for their beloved pet. They finally gave up looking in the dark and hoped she would return home on her own.

By eight o'clock—five hours after Maxine had chased the two girls—the dog was hungry, tired, and scared. She crossed a street without paying attention to the traffic as a car sped around the corner, heading straight for her. At the last moment, the driver slammed on his brakes and the car squealed to a stop. Maxine, her head inches from the front tire, yelped and ran back to the sidewalk. She lowered her head and tail as the driver chewed her out.

Watching from the steps of her apartment building was Amber Post, a twenty-five-year-old secretary. She had held her breath as the scene unfolded, hardly able to watch. When the dog narrowly missed getting hit, Amber sighed with relief. Then she hurried down the steps and called to the frightened animal.

Hearing a soft, friendly voice, Maxine cautiously walked toward the smiling, dark-haired woman. "That's right. Come to me," Amber said.

Maxine sniffed Amber's outstretched hand, then began wagging her tail. Amber stroked the dog's head and noticed she had a collar and a rabies tag. "Are you lost? I'll get the number off your tag and call the animal shelter tomorrow. They should be able to trace your owners."

Amber pulled a fruit bar out of her pocket and held a piece out to the dog. Maxine ate it in one bite.

"You must be hungry. Come with me and I'll see if I can get you some grub."

Maxine followed Amber into the apartment building and up two flights of stairs. The dog dined on leftover pot roast and slurped a big bowl of water.

Just then, Amber's husband, Stuart, came home. "Who is this?" he asked in surprise as Maxine ran to the door, barking.

"I found her in front of the building. She's lost."

"You can't keep her here. You know the rules. The landlord will throw us out."

"It's just for the night, Stu. It's too cold to leave her outside. She has a vaccination tag, so we can call in the morning and find out who her owner is."

Maxine sat down in front of Stuart and broke out into that silly grin of hers.

"Okay. But she's got to be quiet. You know how hard it is to find a decent apartment. We can't afford to get evicted for having a dog here."

"She'll be quiet—I hope."

Amber and Stuart took Maxine for a quick walk before bedtime. After sneaking her back into their apartment, Amber laid a beach towel on the kitchen floor for Maxine to sleep on and closed the door.

On Sunday, the couple usually slept late, but they were awakened by Maxine's frenzied barking at about six in the morning. "Amber, get up," Stuart mumbled, nudging his wife. "That dumb dog is barking like crazy. She's going to wake up the landlord. Shut her up!"

The grumbling woman threw on her robe and shuffled sleepily into the hall. When she walked into the living room, she shrieked. The room was filled with thick smoke. Maxine was yelping and barking, scratching furiously at the closed kitchen door.

"Oh, no! Stu, hurry! The living room's on fire!"

A rug on top of a heat grate had ignited. Amber and Stuart dashed into the kitchen, grabbed pots of water, and doused the small but smoky fire. Then they threw the burned rug out the window.

When the crisis ended, they went into the kitchen and praised Maxine.

"I hate to think what would've happened if this dog hadn't warned us," said Stuart. "Especially since we still haven't replaced the dead battery in our smoke detector."

Minutes later, the landlord knocked on the door. When he learned what had happened, he flew into a rage—over the dog!

"You had a dog in your apartment?" he howled. "That's a blatant violation of the lease. I should throw you two out!"

"But the dog saved our lives—and maybe everyone else's in the building, too," Amber argued.

"She saved your building from going up in flames," Stuart added.

The landlord ignored their words. "No dogs allowed. Get her out of here this instant! I never want to see a dog in this apartment again. Otherwise, you two are out of here for good!"

While Amber took Maxine outside, Stuart called animal control officials, who matched the number on her tag to the Masons. When Stuart called them, they were ecstatic to learn that Maxine was safe—and had saved two more lives.

When the Masons arrived at the apartment building, Maxine, who had been sitting on the steps between Amber and Stuart, let out a joyful wail and jumped on each member of the family.

"We're sad to see her go," said Amber. "Without her, we could have lost our possessions—and our lives."

"Maxine was meant to save us," Stuart declared.

"Yes," added Amber. "Fate led her to us."

Chani pressed her cheek against Maxine's. "You know that old saying 'Where there's smoke, there's fire'? Maybe we should change it to 'Where there's fire, there's Maxine.'"

FOR THE LOVE OF BACON

*C*lick.

Hello? Hello? Is this tape recorder on? I guess so. It's moving inside.

My name is William Duncan, and I want to tell you all about Bacon and how he saved my life. It's important that you know how special he really is.

But first let me tell you about me. I'm twelve years old, and I go to Keith Country Day School. I have two older sisters, Priscilla and Belinda, and they love Bacon too. You can tell I talk kind of slow. Sometimes I have trouble saying the right word. That's because I have Down's syndrome.

Down's syndrome isn't a disease or anything that you can catch. It's something I was born with. My mom said I had two holes in my heart, and the doctor said I wouldn't hear or speak and that I wouldn't be very smart.

Well, guess what? The holes in my heart went away, and I can hear fine. And you can tell I can speak because I'm talking into Priscilla's tape recorder. I'm not brainy like the other kids, but I'm not dumb either. I can write and read and I do my homework. My teacher, Mrs. Gladden, says I'm doing really good.

Sometimes kids say mean things to me and call me a "retard." But they're jerks, and they call other kids bad names too. I have lots of friends who yell back at the jerks. The kids in my class are all nice to me. I think it's because they got to know me. I try to be a nice person and I like everybody. Still, it's hard to like those jerks—and the Halstons, who live behind us. I'll have a lot to say about the Halstons in a little while.

I bet you want to hear about how Bacon saved my life. Let me turn this off because I'm thirsty and I want to get some sweet tea.

Click.

Okay, I'm back. Bacon is the coolest, greatest, neatest pig in the whole world. He belongs to my neighbor Doug Harrison. I'm supposed to call adults like him "Mister," but he told me I should call him Doug, so that's what I do.

When I was nine years old, Doug invited me and Priscilla and Belinda over to see his new pet. I couldn't believe it. It was a pig! But he wasn't a big fat one. He was real tiny. He's what you call a pot-bellied pig.

Doug said he wanted a pot-bellied pig because it doesn't bark like a dog and doesn't scratch the furniture like a cat. I thought he was funny to keep a pig in his house. I asked Doug if he was going to eat the pig. He said, "No, why?" and I said because you get bacon from pigs. Then he said, "That's what I'm going to name him—Bacon." So I got to name his pig.

Bacon is so cute. He's brown and white, and he's got a squished nose and tiny eyes and a tail that wiggles. He's got whiskers, and Priscilla says he's got stubby legs like me.

When Doug first got him, Bacon slept under the bed. He's too big to sleep under the bed now, so he's had his own special place in the basement. He spends the day there while Doug is at work. Bacon sleeps on an old blanket, and he likes to tear up newspapers. I think he gets bored. I know I would if I had to stay in the basement all day. Maybe he should stay outside more.

I go over to Doug's house and play with Bacon. Boy, is he smart. You tell him to sit and he sits. You tell him to come and he comes. He can roll over, too. Wait until you see him dance. It's so funny! He jiggles forward and then back. And he knows how to open kitchen cabinets. Doug said he had to put bug killer and other bad things in a higher place so Bacon wouldn't get them.

Sometimes Doug lets me feed Bacon. He eats pig

chow that Doug buys in a big bag. It's okay to feed Bacon things like apples and corn and carrots, too. He eats right out of my hand, but he gets slobber all over me.

I like the way Bacon grunts when he's happy. He says, "Nof, nof, nof." I think that's his way of saying everything is cool. When he's mad, he lets you know it. He squeals real loud.

Bacon doesn't like cold weather. So if he's left out for very long, he'll come back in and tip over his litter box. Sometimes he gets angry when he has to come inside on a nice day. He likes to poke around in the yard. He sticks his nose in the grass and garden. He looks for worms and stuff like that.

Bacon likes me to scratch his back. He will sit on his fat belly and close his eyes. Sometimes he rolls over and lets me rub his tummy.

When he was little, Bacon used to sit in my lap while we watched TV. He's not real cuddly or soft. He has itchy hair and his feet are real hard.

I got to go to the doctor's with Doug and Bacon in the car. People in other cars were pointing at us. It's like they never saw a pig in a car before. Bacon kept sticking his nose out the back window. He goes to the doctor because he needs a shot so he doesn't get sick. He needs to have his eyes and ears cleaned too. He doesn't like to go to the doctor's. He's always squealing there.

Doug takes Bacon for walks, and sometimes he lets

me hold the leash. People point at us and shout and smile. They think it's funny to walk a pig. I do too. One time, when Bacon was still small, I was walking him, and Mr. Olson, my neighbor down the block, said, "William, that's the ugliest dog I've ever seen!" I laughed and laughed. Then I had to tell him Bacon was a pig. Mr. Olson said, "Maybe he is, but he's still ugly!" Mr. Olson likes to joke a lot.

The best part about taking Bacon for a walk in the summertime is to watch him swim in the pond at the park two streets over from here. He loves the water. He runs right in. He snorts the whole time, and his tail flip-flops back and forth. His little legs go real fast, and he looks like he's running in the water. People stop what they're doing and watch him. When Bacon gets out, everyone claps for him. I think he likes the attention.

Sometimes I feel sad because I don't know how to swim. I'm kind of afraid of the water. But if a pig can swim, I think I could too.

Wait. Belinda just shouted that it's dinnertime. I'll tell you what a hero Bacon is when I'm done eating.

Click.
We had ham for dinner on the same day that I'm talking about Bacon to you on the tape recorder! I know ham comes from pigs, but they're not the kind you keep for pets. They're not pot-bellied pigs like Bacon.

Let's see. What do I want to say next? I try to like everybody, but some people make me mad. I can't help it, but I don't like the Halstons. They live behind us, and they're always making trouble for Bacon and Doug.

The Halstons hate—oops, I'm not supposed to use that word. They really, really don't like Bacon. They're always yelling at him even though he's never done anything to them. He doesn't go in their yard. He sniffs around their fence, but so what?

The Halstons said Bacon is a farm pig and a farm pig doesn't belong in the city. They called the mayor's office and said that Bacon stinks and draws flies and should be sent away. A man came out to Doug's house and told him that he would have to get rid of Bacon. And Doug said, "No way. Bacon is my pet."

So then the man told Doug that he would have to go to court and the judge could take Bacon away and make Doug pay lots of money. Doug said he would fight for his rights. It's true that you can't have a farm animal like a horse or cow in the city. But Bacon isn't a farm animal. He's a pet, a pot-bellied pig.

Bacon is the best pig in the whole world. He saved my life.

Maybe you heard about it. A month ago, I was down at the pond with my mother. We were having a picnic by ourselves. My friend Lucy came over and showed me a toy sailboat that her uncle made. We went down by the pond to sail it. I took my shoes and socks off and went in the water just a little bit. The boat sailed real good.

But then it sailed past Lucy and me and went out into the pond. It was going toward the dock, so I thought I could get it. I got out of the pond and ran to the end of the dock. Then I got on my belly and leaned way over. I could almost touch the sailboat. I stretched out just a little bit more. But I leaned over too much and I fell into the water.

Remember I told you I couldn't swim? I went under real fast, and I swallowed a whole lot of water. I was scared. I was kicking and waving my arms. Finally I came to the top and got to breathe. I shouted for help, but then I went back under.

I heard my mother scream, but she doesn't know how to swim either. But guess what? Bacon came to the rescue!

Doug was walking Bacon by the pond when I fell in. Bacon must have heard me yelling because he yanked the leash out of Doug's hand and ran into the pond. He swam right to me. I didn't see him at first because I was under water. I splashed around real hard and got back to the top for some air. And then I saw Bacon in the water.

My mother was yelling at me to grab Bacon's leash, but I couldn't find it before I went back down. I could see Bacon above me. I was getting real scared because I couldn't breathe and I was very tired. But I kept kicking and went back up again. This time, I got lots of air, and then I saw the leash and grabbed it. I didn't mean to, but I pulled Bacon underwater.

He's a strong pig, and he swam to the top. Then he pulled me into the shallow part. I was so tired I couldn't stand up. But Doug was already in the pond. He carried me out and put me down in the grass.

I was coughing and crying, and my mother was crying, and there were people all around me. I tried to reach out and hug Bacon, but he got pushed out of the way. I swallowed a lot of water, so they took me to the hospital in an ambulance with a real loud siren. That scared me. But I was fine.

When I got home, Doug came over with Bacon. My mom and dad and sisters and I all hugged and hugged that pig. I think Bacon liked that a lot. He kept going, "Nof, nof, nof," like he was real happy and proud of saving my life. I think I would've drowned without Bacon.

The next day there was a big story on the front page of the newspaper and it said, "Hog Hero." Bacon's picture was there, too. I cut it out and hung it up on my wall.

I don't want Bacon to leave. He belongs with Doug because he's a good pig and everybody loves him. Well, everybody but the Halstons. And the Cramers aren't too crazy about him either. But they aren't too crazy about any pets.

My sister Priscilla and I went around the neighborhood asking people to sign their names on a

. . . oh, what's the word? . . . a *petition* to let Doug keep Bacon. Lots of people signed it. We didn't bother going to the Halstons or the Cramers.

Doug said what we did was really nice and he thanked us. I think Bacon understood, because he gave me a big kiss. Doug said the petition might help him convince the judge to let Bacon stay. He asked me if I would answer some questions in court. I wanted to help Bacon because he helped me. Mom and Dad said it was all right if I went to court. They even let me skip school.

I had never been in a courtroom before. The judge was nice. The Halstons and Cramers were there too. I didn't understand everything that people said. The Halstons said some mean things about Bacon, and some other people I'd never seen before said that farm animals can't live in the city. One man said a pot-bellied pig is a farm animal. He also said something that got me real mad. He said it didn't matter that Bacon was a hero. Well, it matters to me. I wouldn't be talking to you if it wasn't for Bacon.

I wanted to tell the judge how nice and sweet Bacon is and how he saved my life. But the judge wouldn't let me. He let Doug talk. Afterward, the judge took a day to decide.

You probably know what happened. The judge said Bacon was a farm animal and couldn't stay. I cried real hard when Mom told me. She said Doug could go to jail if he kept Bacon. That's just not fair.

I went over to say good-bye to Bacon. I gave him an apple, and then I cried. Doug told me it would be all right because he found a good home for Bacon out in the country. He said you are a very kind lady because you take care of other pigs when they can't live in the city anymore. I hope Bacon makes lots of pig friends. He has lots of human friends here.

I'm making this tape for you so you know how special Bacon is. Don't forget, he saved my life. I'm sure going to miss him. Doug said he will take me out to your place to visit Bacon.

Please be extra nice to him. He likes his back scratched and his tummy rubbed. His favorite treat is popcorn without the butter. You will remember, won't you?

Click.

THE LITTLE HORSE THAT COULD

"So, honey, what would you like for your birthday?" Linda Dawson asked her daughter, Heather, at the dinner table.

"A horse, of course!" declared Heather. "I'll take care of him every day. I'll feed him and brush him. We've got enough pasture for him. Please? It would be the perfect present for my thirteenth birthday."

"Now, Heather," said her father, Dave. "We've gone over this before. I know how much you love horses. Your room is a corral for every kind of horse— carved, ceramic, plastic, porcelain, stuffed, glass. But a real horse is simply out of the question. We can't afford to care for one. Besides, you get to ride Sprite every Saturday." Sprite belonged to John and Martha Long, who were neighbors and close friends of the Dawsons.

"That's not the same as having my own."

"I'm sorry, honey. How about a trail bike?"

Heather wrinkled her round, freckled face and smiled halfheartedly. "Daddy, I'd be happy with anything you gave me."

"If we could afford it, you'd have your horse. I'm sorry."

Afterward, Heather helped her mother with the dishes. "Didn't you like dinner?" Linda asked. "You hardly ate anything."

"Your fried chicken was great, Mom. I just wasn't hungry."

"Is it because you're upset over not getting a horse?"

"It has nothing to do with a horse."

"Then what is it, Heather? Why aren't you eating?"

"I'm trying to cut back. Lately I've noticed I'm getting wider around the middle, and I can't fit into my clothes."

"Look, young lady, you must eat a well-balanced diet. Now don't you worry about your waistline. You're short and stocky like me. I don't want you to starve yourself trying to stay thin."

"I won't. I promise."

The next morning, Heather woke up with such severe pains in her stomach that she was taken to the hospital. A series of tests revealed the worst news of all—she had a cancerous tumor the size of a football in her stomach.

After the tumor was removed, Heather underwent

chemotherapy that left her physically weak. It also caused her hair to fall out, so she wore a baseball cap to cover her bald head. She endured long days in the hospital and suffered awful side effects from the treatment, such as nausea and aching muscles.

But there was at least one good thing to come out of her ordeal—Smurf.

While Heather was in the hospital, an agency dedicated to brightening the lives of seriously ill children asked her to list three wishes on a form. Heather didn't hesitate. On each of the three lines, she wrote one word in big letters—HORSE.

Heather didn't have much hope that her wish would come true. But one day, during her recovery at home, she and her parents received a lunch invitation from the Longs.

When the Dawsons arrived, Martha told Heather, "There's someone I want you to meet. She's in the barn."

Heather, followed by her parents and the Longs, walked into the barn. Next to Sprite's stall stood a skinny, reddish-brown quarter horse mare, much smaller than Sprite. The animal snorted and stuck her nose over the stall gate.

"Well, hello there," Heather cooed. The horse responded with another snort, then nuzzled her nose against Heather's cheek. "I like you too." Turning to Martha, Heather said, "She's sweet but she doesn't look very healthy."

"She's malnourished because her previous owner

didn't look after her. She's going to need lots of tender, loving care."

"I'll be glad to help you out, Martha."

"It won't be necessary to help *me* out," said Martha. She paused and winked at Linda.

Heather's mother grinned and explained, "You see, Heather, this horse is yours."

Heather stopped stroking the horse's forehead. "Mine? What do you mean?"

"I mean, she is your very own horse!"

Tears of happiness trickled down Heather's face. "Oh, thank you, thank you," she cried, embracing her parents and the Longs. "But I thought you said it was too expensive."

"Under the circumstances, we figured we'd find a way to afford her upkeep," said Dave. "The Longs are nice enough to let us board her here."

"Where did you get her?"

"She came from a horse rescue league that finds new owners for abused or neglected animals," replied Linda. "Remember when you were in the hospital and the children's agency asked what you wished for? Well, they went to the rescue league and found this mare. She spent the first three years of her life without proper food or medical care. But in spite of that, she has a sweet personality."

"What do you want to call her?" asked Dave.

"She's small for her age, so I'll call her Smurf." Upon hearing the name, the horse whinnied and stomped her foot. "I think Smurf likes her new name!"

While caring for Smurf, Heather made a full recovery—and so did the horse. With their health restored, they formed an exceptionally close bond.

Heather often rode Smurf into the nearby woods and pastures. The teen would talk to her horse about school, boys, and the future.

Before each ride, Heather made a point of telling someone where she and Smurf would be. One day after school, she saddled up Smurf. Because no one was around, Heather dutifully wrote a note and nailed it to the door of Smurf's stable. "Took the pond trail. Left at four. Be back by six. Heather."

Because of heavy rains, it had been nearly a week since Heather had last ridden Smurf. The trail was quite muddy, but neither horse nor rider seemed to mind. They were outdoors—and, more important, they were together.

At a clearing about halfway to the pond, Heather spotted a large, dark bird with a white head and white tail soaring overhead. "Whoa, Smurf. I think that's a bald eagle. Wow, that's beautiful!"

The eagle glided high in the air, emitting piercing screams. Then it dove behind a stand of poplar trees that bordered the north side of the pond. Moments later, the eagle zoomed above the tree line. "Look, Smurf. It's got a fish in its claws. Let's follow it. Maybe it will take us to its nest."

They turned off the pond trail and followed the

magnificent bird toward a rocky area known as the Ledges. Two angled cliffs rose on either side of a narrow valley strewn with large rocks torn from the slopes by heavy rains over the centuries. It was a bleak area that few people bothered to visit because there were no easy trails.

When Smurf and Heather arrived at the Ledges, the horse carefully picked her way through the rocky rubble as her rider scanned the cliffs looking for the eagle's nest. With the late afternoon sun lighting up the eastern bluff, Heather saw the eagle standing majestically on its huge cliffside nest about one hundred feet (30.5 m) above the ground.

"Oh, look! There's an eaglet in the nest! It's eating the fish her daddy brought."

Unexpectedly, Smurf started acting up. She whinnied, stomped her feet, and bobbed her head. "What's wrong, girl? Is something out there?" Heather quickly checked the ground for snakes, but she didn't see any. She looked for any coyotes, wolves, or mountain lions lurking behind boulders.

Just then, she heard a rumble and a loud thud. Glancing behind her, she saw a rock the size of a microwave oven tumbling down the side of the western cliff. Smurf's ears twitched forward—a sure sign that she was frightened.

Leaning over her mount's neck, Heather soothingly told Smurf, "Calm down, girl. It's all right. It's only a falling rock. No big deal."

The rock bounced to a stop about a hundred yards (91 m) from them. Smurf reared up while Heather struggled to maintain control. "Hey, take it easy, Smurf. Maybe it's not such a good idea to stay here. With all the rain we've had, some of those rocks could slide down the cliffs. Let's go."

As she turned the horse around, the ground began to shake and a thunderous roar echoed through the valley. Seconds later huge chunks of the bluff crashed down the side. "Rock slide!" Heather screamed.

She kicked Smurf in the ribs and tried to get out of the way of the deadly rock fall. Enormous boulders bounded into the valley, each weighing more than enough to crush a horse and its rider.

"Hurry, Smurf! Hurry!" By the time Heather had uttered the command, the rocks had hit the valley floor and crashed into other boulders. Smurf was valiantly making her way through the obstacle course when a rock the size of a television set slammed into her right front leg. Her limb buckled and she fell in a heap, pitching Heather forward. The girl was hurled onto a large slab of shale.

Heather then heard a sickening snap in her right leg. Wincing from the jabbing pain, she knew she had broken her leg. She lay in a pile of dust with small stones scattered over her prone body. When she tried to squirm free, pain shot up her right leg, which was pinned by a fallen rock. Her ribs were so sore, it was hard to breathe.

Heather leaned against a boulder. "Smurf, Smurf," she whispered. "Are you here? Are you okay?" Unable to twist her body, she craned her neck. Off to her left stood her horse. Smurf whinnied but didn't move.

"Oh, Smurf. Thank goodness you're safe!" Then she saw a bloody six-inch (15-cm) gash in the horse's right leg. Smurf looked terrified. "You poor thing. You're hurt. So am I." Fighting off panic, Heather said, "I feel like crying, Smurf, but that isn't going to do us any good. We're in a bad mess. I'm trapped and you've got an injured leg. What's worse, no one will start looking for us for another hour or two. And when they do, they'll be searching the pond trail because that's where I said we'd be. They won't come to the Ledges, at least not for a while. You know, I think I'm going to cry anyway." Heather broke down, but she had to stifle her sobs because each one hurt her ribs.

When she regained her composure, she motioned for Smurf. "Come here, girl. Can you walk? Come to me." Smurf snorted. Keeping her injured leg off the ground, the horse limped through the rubble to reach Heather.

"Smurf, I need you to do me a big favor. The stable is a mile (1.6 km) away. It'll be dark in about two hours. You've got to go back and get help."

Heather took off the fanny pack she wore around her waist. She had no paper or pencil to write a message. Instead, she picked up a piece of shale—a rock formed of hard clay that splits easily into thin layers. It was quite common in the Ledges. She placed it in her fanny pack, then buckled the pack to one of Smurf's stirrups.

"I hope when Mom and Dad find this in my fanny pack, they'll know I'm at the Ledges and not the pond. The rest is up to you, Smurf. Go home! Go home!"

The horse snorted but didn't budge.

"I know you're hurting and bleeding badly, but you've got to get help. You don't need to stay with me. Please go home!"

Smurf backed up and whinnied. Then she hobbled a few feet and stopped. "Go on home, Smurf. Get going!"

Smurf snorted and hobbled in the direction of the barn. *I hope I did the right thing by sending her off. Am I being selfish? What if she bleeds to death because I made her walk back?* Heather began crying again.

Heather's worried parents arrived at the Longs' farm at seven that evening. "Is my daughter back yet?" asked Dave.

"I'm afraid not," replied Martha.

"Something terrible must have happened," Linda fretted. "Heather would never be this late."

"John is saddling up Sprite right now to go look for her on the pond trail," said Martha. Pointing to their four-wheeled all-terrain vehicle, she suggested, "Why don't you take our ATV?"

"We'd better hurry," Dave said. "There's only about an hour of daylight left."

"Look!" shouted Linda. She pointed to a horse limping toward them from the shadows of the trees. "It's Smurf. But where's Heather?"

"Smurf is hurt!" gasped Martha. The horse, exhausted and in obvious pain, sat on her rump and rolled over on her left side. "Her leg is bleeding badly."

Dave ran to the horse and found Heather's fanny pack buckled to the stirrup. "Maybe there's a note inside." He unzipped it and pulled out the rock. "It's a piece of shale. Heather doesn't collect rocks." Seconds later, he snapped his fingers. "Of course, shale is all over the Ledges. Her note said she was taking the pond trail, but she must have changed her mind. She's probably hurt somewhere in the Ledges. Let's go!"

"I'll call the sheriff's office and tell them to send an emergency unit," Martha said. "And I'll call Dr. James to tend to Smurf. She's one gutsy horse. Let's hope her effort will lead you to Heather."

Twenty minutes later, the two men reached the Ledges and began shouting Heather's name. Her bruised ribs made it difficult for Heather to shout back loudly enough to be heard. In desperation, she grabbed a small rock and banged it against the boulder.

"Over here!" she said weakly.

The men heard her striking the rock. "Heather, is that you?" shouted her father. "Keep hitting the rock."

They quickly found the trapped, pain-racked girl. "Daddy, John, am I glad to see you!"

"How badly are you hurt?" asked Dave.

"It hurts to breathe or talk, and I can't move my right leg. It's broken. We got caught in a rock slide."

"We'll get you out of here real soon," John assured her.

"How did you find me?"

"Smurf," Dave replied. "She made it back to the barn. It was pretty smart of you to put a piece of shale in your fanny pack. When I saw that rock, I figured you were at the Ledges."

Girdling the boulder with a chain from the ATV, the men moved the big rock and freed Heather, then rushed her back to the farm. But she refused to go into the waiting ambulance until she saw Smurf first.

Dr. James discovered that the tendons—tissues that connect the muscle to the bone—in Smurf's injured leg had been cut. "I don't know how she managed to walk back with this injury," the vet said. "Pure guts and determination. But she's very weak from loss of blood."

As Heather was lifted onto a stretcher, she squeezed the vet's arm and pleaded, "Save her, doctor, save her."

After Heather left, Dr. James told the Dawsons, "I hate to say this, but you may want to have this horse put down to end her suffering."

"We can't do that," Linda declared. "Not after what she did for Heather. Smurf is very special. She saved my daughter's life. There's no way we'd have Smurf put to sleep."

"She'll need to be immobilized in a sling for a month," said the vet. "Then she must stay in her stall for another month before she can begin to walk. Do you think you can handle that?"

"Somehow we'll manage," said Dave. "Heather and Smurf have gone through so much together, we can't let them down now."

Dr. James put fifty stitches in Smurf's leg and rigged up a sling to keep her from using her damaged limb.

Heather and Smurf kept each other company as their injured legs slowly healed. The Dawsons borrowed the Longs' ATV so Heather could make the trip from her home to the stable every afternoon. After her cast came off, Heather used a cane and began to walk Smurf from one end of the barn to the other.

Finally, three months after the accident, a wonderful day arrived. "Look, Smurf," Heather announced when she arrived at the stable. "No cane!"

Smurf bobbed her head and snorted her approval. "Now it's your turn." Heather led the horse out of the barn and into a small pen for the first time since the injury. "I want you to walk by yourself, nice and easy."

Smurf took a few steady steps and whinnied. Then she began to run and buck back and forth in the pen, releasing months of pent-up energy. And she did it all without a limp.

"We've done it, Smurf!" Heather crowed, clapping her hands. "Once again, we've come back from the hard times. Now we're ready for the good times!"

THE GENTLE GIANTS

"I don't want to see the gorillas, Grandpa," whimpered Kevin Morris. The pint-sized six-year-old held tight to Henry Bowles's hand as they strolled with Kevin's older brother, Mark, and his grandmother, Celeste, toward the exhibit in the animal park. "Gorillas scare me."

Henry had hoped this trip would change the little boy's anxiety about the hulking primates. Kevin had a real but unfounded fear of the gorillas. It started when Kevin and Mark saw a horror movie about killer gorillas on cable TV. Mark, a natural-born troublemaker, knew Kevin was scared, and he inspired even more terror with wild tales of man-eating gorillas. Ever since then, Kevin couldn't even look at photographs of gorillas without freaking out.

"Gorillas are mean," Kevin told his grandfather.

"No, they're not. They are among the most gentle, shy creatures on this planet. I'll prove it to you."

Henry didn't need to prove it. Two gorillas did it for him.

Kevin and Mark were from a small town in Virginia. They were staying with their grandparents near London, England, for a week while their parents were on a bicycling tour of France.

Henry and Celeste had no idea what they were getting into when they agreed to watch the boys for the week. Grandpa and Grammy were constantly breaking up squabbles, usually triggered by Mark, a husky nine-year-old whose favorite sport was bullying his little brother.

At the animal park, Mark asked in his most innocent voice, "Can we see the gorillas now?" He knew the request would scare his brother. "Come on, please?"

"Let's see the lions first," Kevin suggested. He was hoping that if they saw all the other animals there wouldn't be time for the gorillas.

"What's the matter, Kevin?" taunted Mark. "Are you afraid of some overgrown monkeys?" Mark hopped around, doing a poor imitation of an ape.

"That's enough, Mark," Henry ordered. Henry was a college professor, so he tried to ease Kevin's fears by presenting some facts about the animal. Unfortunately, Henry went into his lecturing mode—

a dry monotone that did little to comfort or reassure the young boy.

"Gorillas come from tropical West Africa," he explained. "They really are quite friendly. They live in groups of five to fifteen, usually with at least one silverback. He's called that because he has gray or silver hair on his back. The silverback is often the oldest and strongest of the group, so he's the leader.

"Gorillas spend the day playing, napping, and eating berries and leaves. They certainly don't go around attacking people."

"But I've seen big gorillas pounding their chests and making noise on TV," said Kevin.

"The male gorilla beats his chest from time to time," answered Henry. "He does it to scare anyone or anything that gets near the females and babies. He's protecting them from possible harm.

"Gorillas have no natural enemies, but they are in danger of extinction because of man's thought-lessness. It's really a tragedy.

"The gorilla compound is up ahead. Let's go there next." Henry felt resistance in Kevin's hand. "It'll be fine. You'll see."

The viewing area looked down on a large compound dotted with boulders, plants, and a shallow pond and ringed by a twenty-foot-high (6-m) man-made cliff. With his grandfather's encouragement, Kevin walked to the edge of the viewing area and took a quick peek. He jumped back quickly.

"You didn't even look," Mark sneered. "I bet you can't even tell me how many gorillas there are."

"I didn't count them. Maybe ten or twelve."

Mark looked down into the compound. A silverback was munching on sweet potatoes, two smaller gorillas were napping, and two females were grooming their babies.

"There are only seven," said Mark. "Take a good look, or are you a chicken?" Mark tucked his hands under his armpits, flapped his elbows, and squawked.

"Stop that tomfoolery!" Henry snapped. "If there's any more trouble from either of you, we'll leave."

Henry turned away from the boys when Celeste called him over to say hello to some old friends who were walking by.

"You're a jerk," Kevin said to his brother as soon as his grandfather was out of earshot.

"Oh, yeah?" Mark swiped the Baltimore Orioles cap off Kevin's head and held the cap up so Kevin couldn't grab it back.

Kevin knew if he whined or complained, their day at the zoo would end. Instead, he quietly pleaded with his brother. "Gimme it, Mark. That's my favorite hat."

Letting the cap dangle from his finger high over Kevin, Mark snarled, "It's yours if you can get it."

Kevin leaped up and swatted the hat just as a gust of wind whipped it onto the limb of a tree growing in the compound. The hat hung on a branch an arm's length from the viewing area's three-foot-high (.9-m) stone-and-bamboo barrier. Mark laughed and walked away, pretending nothing had happened.

Kevin knew he needed to get his cap before his grandparents saw him. He climbed onto the barrier. Not wanting to look down at the gorillas, he turned his head away and groped for the cap, leaning over as far as he dared.

At that moment, Celeste saw her grandson, his arm outstretched, teetering on top of the barrier. "Kevin! No!" she screamed.

Her yell startled the boy so much, he lost his balance. He flipped over the barrier, caromed off a ledge jutting out from the fake cliff, and landed on a cement drainage area inside the gorilla compound.

Henry dashed over to the barrier and looked down. His stomach twisted at the sight of Kevin lying unconscious, sprawled on his back, his limbs at odd angles like a broken doll's.

In the compound, Bwana, a four-hundred-pound (180-kg), five-foot-eight-inch (1.7-m) silverback and leader of the gorillas, hopped off his perch the moment he saw something fall to the ground. He ambled close to the motionless boy and uttered a hooting sound—a signal of alarm.

Sitting down near Kevin, Bwana touched the boy, then jerked his finger away. When Kevin didn't move, the gorilla inched closer and poked the boy again. Seeing no response, the silverback crouched next to Kevin and lifted the boy's arm as if looking for signs of life. Kevin's arm flopped across his chest.

Up above in the viewing area, a hushed crowd watched spellbound as Bwana carefully examined the boy. Celeste was too shocked to look.

"The gorilla acts as if he's wondering if your grandson is okay," Celeste's friend told her.

"He's not going to hurt Kevin, is he?" Celeste asked.

"No, you can tell he wants to help."

Unfortunately, the caretakers for the gorillas were on a break at the time of the accident. In the compound, the other gorillas—some grunting and barking in surprise over this unexpected incident— cautiously headed toward the fallen boy. When he saw them, Bwana turned his back to Kevin and stood up. Then he protectively let out several sharp grunts—a clear signal to the others to stay away. Like an adult silverback in the wild, Bwana was keeping order in his group and protecting the young—even if the young was a human.

By now, Kevin had regained consciousness. The woozy boy tried to raise himself, but his head hurt too much. "Where am I?" he whined. "What happened?"

He looked up and saw a throng of strange but concerned faces gawking down at him from the viewing area. Then he recognized his grandfather. "Kevin, don't move!" shouted Henry. "Help will be there in a few minutes!"

Now it was all coming back to Kevin. *Mark swiped*

my cap . . . it flew into the tree . . . I tried to get it . . . Grammy screamed . . . I fell into the gorillas' pit!

Suddenly, a shadow loomed over him. Kevin stared up at large, flaring nostrils and big, dark eyes under a protruding brow, all set against a black face.

It was Bwana. To Kevin, the face might as well have belonged to Dracula or Frankenstein's monster. Inches away from the one animal he feared the most, the horror-stricken boy let out a shrill wail that sent Bwana jumping backward. Although it hurt to cry, Kevin bawled in terror.

"Kevin!" shouted Henry. "Stay calm. Don't cry or make any noise! The gorilla won't harm you if you stay quiet. You're scaring him!"

"But he's scaring me!" Kevin whimpered.

The silverback stood up, advanced toward Kevin, and let out a nasty growl. "He's going to hurt me!" Kevin wailed.

But Bwana didn't harm the boy. Instead, the gorilla's anger had been directed at another male sneaking up to Kevin from the side. After shooing him away, Bwana sat down, his back to the boy, and glared at the other gorillas.

For the first time, Kevin sensed that the silverback wanted to protect him. The other gorillas tried to creep closer to Kevin, but Bwana kept all of them at bay—all except one.

A young mother named Kumba approached Kevin but backed away when Bwana growled at her. She stared at Bwana for a moment, then boldly shuffled past him to the trembling boy.

"Not another gorilla," Kevin mumbled fearfully. "Go away! Please, go away!"

Cocking her head to one side, Kumba leaned over and touched Kevin's bleeding head. The boy's heart was beating so wildly, it hurt.

Meanwhile, the zookeepers had hooked up hoses and were spraying four gorillas that had gathered several yards from the injured boy. The hoses weren't trained on Bwana and Kumba because of concern that the high-powered spray would harm Kevin.

While the other gorillas scattered, Kumba sat down and gently put her arms under Kevin's. "What are you doing?" the boy whined. "Don't hurt me!"

Kumba tenderly placed him in her lap. Then, as she had done with her own child, she cradled his head in her arms. Kevin's pain disappeared, along with his fear. He felt the warmth and gentleness of the mother gorilla's arms. Her itchy brown hair and strong body odor didn't matter to him. He wasn't scared anymore.

Kevin lay still, sensing a compassion strangely similar to what he felt when his mother held him. But his fear returned when Kumba and Bwana made loud grunting noises. He felt her body tense. Then Kumba carefully pushed Kevin off her lap. She got up and moved away. So did Bwana.

Turning his head, Kevin saw that the zookeepers were advancing and trying to drive off the two gorillas.

Meanwhile, a stretcher was being lowered from above. Within minutes, a paramedic rappelled down the cliff and placed Kevin on the stretcher. The boy was pulled to the top and taken to the hospital, where he was treated for a concussion, a head wound that needed twenty stitches, and a broken wrist.

After a day in the hospital, Kevin returned to his grandparents' apartment to recover. Before leaving for Virginia, Kevin insisted on going back to the animal park to thank the gorillas.

The zoo's director, Virgil Fitzsimmons, escorted Kevin and his family to the viewing area of the gorilla compound. Mr. Fitzsimmons was happy to be able to return Kevin's baseball cap. Kevin fondly gazed at the magnificent primates. Bwana was playing with his favorite toy—a fifty-gallon (190-l) plastic barrel. Kumba was grooming Shala, her eighteen-month-old daughter.

Kevin waved and shouted, "Hi, Bwana! Hi, Kumba! Thanks!" The two gorillas looked up and uttered low growls, then went back to their activities.

"Those growls express pleasure," explained Fitzsimmons. "We can't be sure what was going on in their minds when you fell, Kevin. But Bwana is the father of five, and it seems that his instinct to protect someone young is quite strong. Kumba is a first-time mother. When she became pregnant we were afraid she wouldn't know how to be a mother, so trainers used a stuffed doll to teach her to nurse and carry her baby. After Shala was born, Kumba proved to be a great mom. But no one taught Kumba or Bwana how to react to an unconscious boy who fell into their compound."

Henry put his arm around his grandson's shoulder. "How do you feel about gorillas now, Kevin?" he asked.

"They are gentle, just like you said."

When Mark, who was standing behind Henry, began making funny faces at his brother, Kevin said, "Grandpa, I have a question. If gorillas can be so nice to me, why can't my brother?"

ANGELS OF THE SEA

Calisa Mills's heart pounded with excitement and goosebumps rippled her arms. She was so nervous she was afraid she wouldn't be able to breathe through her snorkel.

The eighth-grader from New Jersey was about to realize a lifelong dream—swimming with dolphins. She and her family were on vacation off the northeast coast of Australia. They had hired Captain Joe Baker and his weathered wooden boat to take them to an area several miles offshore where people-friendly dolphins frolicked.

Captain Baker cut the engine. "This is the spot," he announced to Calisa, her fifteen-year-old brother, Brooks, and their parents, Don and Karen. The captain's instructions were simple: "Don't touch the dolphins. If they want to, they will touch you. Swim with your hands at your sides and don't swim directly at them or behind them. If you do, they might think you're about to attack. Try to make eye contact and show them you want to be their friend. Finally, have fun!"

Calisa inhaled through her nose, sucking the mask tightly against her tanned face. She bit down on the mouthpiece of her snorkel and slid off the boat into the shimmering, crystal-clear water.

Within seconds, Calisa heard the wondrous clicks and whirs of the dolphins, but she couldn't see them. Suddenly, a flash of gray and white zipped beneath her. It was a ten-foot-long (3-m) adult dolphin.

As instructed, Calisa dove down and made eye contact with the sleek mammal. She smiled through her face mask and tried her best to send a mental message. *Hi. I'm really happy to meet you. I think you are the most beautiful, most awesome animal in the world. I hope you like me. I want to be your friend.*

As Calisa met the dolphin's steady gaze, she felt he actually understood what she was thinking. His lovable eyes shone with an intelligence she had seen in no other animal.

In her excitement, Calisa forgot that her lungs were screaming for air. *I don't want to leave you, but I've got to get some air. Don't go away. I'll be right back.*

When she broke the surface, Calisa joyfully shouted, "This is so awesome! I can't believe it!"

From the stern of the boat, Captain Baker chuckled. "Enjoy, my young friend. Enjoy these angels of the sea."

Before Calisa had a chance to head down again, two dolphins streaked by her, one on each side, leaving a stream of bubbles in their wake. With her hands by her side, she kicked hard, but the dolphins moved too fast for her to keep up.

They made a U-turn and swam so close to Calisa that she was convinced they would bump into her. *I want to touch them so badly. They seem to like me. Maybe if I pretend to touch them accidentally, they won't mind.* But the moment that thought came into her head, the dolphins sped away. *They can read my mind!* Calisa thought.

Calisa was alone for only a minute before a mother dolphin and her calf circled the enchanted girl. The mother stopped, poked her head out of the water, and stared at her. Treading water, Calisa took off her mask so that the dolphin could get a good look at her. Then the calf stuck his head out too.

"Hi, guys! Nice to meet you. My name is Calisa."

The calf squeaked and shook his head before submerging. His mother joined him and the two began swimming slowly away. Calisa put on her mask, adjusted her snorkel and slipped under the water.

Suddenly, Calisa felt a strange jolt, almost like a mild electrical shock. It startled her so much that she stopped swimming and returned to the surface, bewildered by the odd sensation.

The mother dolphin surfaced, too, and opened her mouth, exposing dozens of cone-shaped teeth in a dolphin smile. Then she and her calf swam off.

Back on the boat, the elated Mills family breathlessly shared their dolphin experiences with each other. When Calisa mentioned that she'd felt a slight electrical shock, the captain applauded. "Ah, you're so fortunate. The mother dolphin echo-located you."

"What's that mean?" she asked.

"The dolphin uses sonar to scan the water. This sonar is incredibly precise. In fact, a dolphin can echo-locate a shark a half mile (.8 k) away and determine whether its stomach is full or empty. If the shark's stomach is empty . . ." Joe stopped, hoping one of the Millses would finish the sentence.

" . . . then the dolphin better stay away from the shark," said Brooks, "because the shark could be hungry, right?"

"Very good!" the captain said. "Calisa, the mother dolphin sent out a sonar signal. That's what you felt. She must have found something quite interesting about you."

"Yeah," Brooks piped up, "the dolphin probably never saw such a weird-looking human before!"

He laughed and then ducked when Calisa flung her mask at him. "Not even your dumb remark is going to ruin this day," she said.

The old wooden boat was chugging back to port when an agitated dolphin began crisscrossing in front of the bow. Several times he swam under the boat and then came up on the other side, squeaking loudly.

Captain Baker stepped away from the wheel and peered over the side. "I'm not sure why he's doing that. Maybe he wants us to follow him. It's not uncommon for a dolphin to guide ships. Let me tell you about Pelorus Jack. He was one of the most famous dolphins ever because he saved an untold number of lives.

"Pelorus Jack lived many years ago, long before ships had the sophisticated electronic gear they use today. He was named after the pelorus, a device used for navigation.

"This amazing dolphin lived in the waters off New Zealand in a channel known as French Pass. This channel is extremely hazardous because it's full of rocks and has very strong currents. Why, I can't tell you how many ships have been wrecked in French Pass—hundreds, maybe thousands. But no ship was ever wrecked when Pelorus Jack was at work."

Joe stroked his bushy red beard. "Is that dolphin still in front of us?"

"Yes," said Brooks. "I hope we don't run over him."

"Ah, mate, there's no chance of that. Now, on with my story. PJ—that's what I call Pelorus Jack—was first seen by the sailors of the Boston schooner called the *Brindle*. As the ship entered French Pass, PJ appeared at the bow just like that dolphin is doing right now.

One of the crewmen got out a gun. He wanted to shoot the dolphin.

"Fortunately, the captain's wife gave the sailor a tongue-lashing and he put away his gun. PJ then guided the ship through that narrow channel with no problem. For years thereafter, PJ safely led many other ships through French Pass.

"He was so dependable that when ships reached French Pass, the sailors would look for him. If they didn't see him, the ship would circle outside the channel and wait for him to show up. That's how good he was.

"One day, a ship named the *Penguin* entered French Pass. A stupid passenger pulled out a gun and shot PJ. The dolphin was bleeding badly and swam off. The crew was so furious, they nearly lynched the passenger. Fortunately, the *Penguin* managed to make it safely through French Pass without PJ's help.

"No one saw PJ for several weeks, and the sailors assumed that he had died. Other ships had to navigate through the treacherous waters without his help. But one day, PJ showed up and began guiding ships again. He had recovered and was willing to forgive the humans—most of them.

"You see, the next time the *Penguin* entered French Pass, PJ disappeared under the water. The ship had to manage on its own. For several more years, PJ helped other ships get through the channel, but he never would guide the *Penguin*. Finally, the ship was wrecked on some shoals in French Pass and sank, taking dozens of passengers and crewmen to their deaths."

Calisa leaned over the bow to watch the dolphin. He continued to jump in front of the boat, squeaking and shaking his head. "Captain," she asked, "do you think this dolphin is trying to tell us something?"

Joe walked over to the bow and pondered the scene. "It seems like he wants us to stop this boat," he said.

After the captain cut off the engine, the dolphin crisscrossed the bow, stuck his head out of the water, squeaked, and snorted through his blow hole. "I better take a look under the boat," said Joe. He fitted himself with a snorkel, mask, and fins and jumped in.

Captain Baker examined the bow while the dolphin circled nearby. After several minutes, Joe climbed aboard and said, "Would you believe that dolphin was warning us of a problem?"

"What is it?" asked Calisa's father.

"There's a crack in the bow. It needs my quick attention or else we'll all be taking an unscheduled—and quite long—swim." The captain went below deck and saw water leaking through the crack. He cranked up a pump to suck out the water and smeared the crack from the inside with a special repair plaster. "That'll hold until we get back to the marina," he declared. "No need to worry."

"Did the dolphin save us from sinking?" Brooks asked.

"That's quite possible, son."

Calisa scanned the horizon, looking for the dolphin, but he had left. "We didn't even get to say thank you. I can't wait to get back home and tell everyone that we were saved by a dolphin."

She soon would have an even better—and more terrifying—story to tell.

Two days after the Millses swam with the dolphins, they chartered a forty-foot (12-m) yacht for a weekend of exploring along the Great Barrier Reef. The Reef is the largest coral formation in the world, stretching more than 1,250 miles (2,012 km) off the Australian state of Queensland.

The yacht, skippered by Calisa's father, soon came upon a pod of about twenty dolphins. "Are they rounding up a school of fish?" Brooks wondered out loud.

"No, I think they're racing toward the boat to greet us!" Calisa replied excitedly.

The dolphins swam alongside the sailboat, body-surfing the waves as the Mills family whooped and hollered. Occasionally, one of the dolphins would swim on its side and gaze at them in a friendly way. "Daddy, can we please stop and swim with the dolphins?" Calisa begged.

Her father eyed the sky, which was rapidly darkening with threatening clouds. "We can't stop here. We need to get to a protected area before this storm hits." Within the hour, they had anchored in a bay ringed on three sides by coral shoals. The storm soon hit, rocking the sailboat with strong gusts and heavy rain.

The next morning dawned quiet and clear. Calisa, the first to rise, walked onto the deck and admired the pinkish glow of the sky. The only sound was the water lapping against the hull. Then her ears detected a faint but distinctive clicking sound. Calisa scurried to the side. Dancing in the water was a young bottlenose dolphin no bigger than she was.

"Hi, sugar!" shouted Calisa. "How are you this morning?"

The little dolphin circled once, then leaped out of the water, returning so perfectly that he hardly made a splash. *I've got to go in*, thought Calisa. *I can't pass up another chance to swim with a dolphin.*

Not even bothering to change into a swimsuit, Calisa quickly grabbed her snorkel, fins, and mask out of the storage box. In her haste, she gashed her arm on the edge of the lid. As her arm started to bleed, she thought, *I don't want to waste any more time. The salt water will wash out the cut.* She jumped overboard.

The dolphin came right toward Calisa, then dipped down. The girl dove after him. Once again, she felt the zapping sensation of echo-location. *Do you like me as much as I like you?* Calisa wondered.

The dolphin moved closer and turned his back to her, waving the dorsal fin on his back. *Do you want me to touch you?* Up to now, Calisa had been careful not to get too close to him. But the dolphin made it clear he wanted her to grab on to his fin. As soon as she did, he took off with Calisa holding on for dear life.

The dolphin dove down about ten feet (3 m), then returned to the surface, allowing Calisa to catch her breath before they went for another underwater ride. *I'm riding on the back of a dolphin!* Calisa marveled. *What a dream—only it's real!*

But the dreamy moment was about to turn horrifying.

The dolphin picked up speed, slipping under the surface and heading out toward the open water. As he dove deeper than before, Calisa's enjoyment turned to concern. *I can't go any farther with you. We're too far away from the boat. Besides, I need air.* She let go and drifted to the surface while the dolphin disappeared.

Calisa realized that she was alone in the water, about a quarter mile (.4 km)—more than the length of four football fields—from the boat. Her arm ached, and she noticed that her gash was deeper than she had thought and still bleeding. But she didn't care. Her mind and heart brimmed with affection and gratitude for her blissful, unforgettable encounter with the little dolphin. Calisa lazily backstroked toward the boat.

Five minutes later, as she rolled over onto her stomach to do the breast stroke, she spotted a dorsal fin. *Oh, good. He came back.* Then Calisa looked more closely and her body tensed with fright. *That's not a dolphin. It's a shark!*

She whirled around, hoping to see an exposed rock that she could reach before the shark came any closer. But the nearest rock was on the other side of the boat.

"Help!" Calisa yelled. "Dad! Mom! Brooks! Shark!" She began to shake in terror as the shark, smelling the blood from her cut arm, zeroed in on his prey. *I'm going to get eaten alive!*

Calisa had never felt so alone, so helpless. She screamed for help until her throat burned. But her family continued to sleep soundly below deck. The shark circled Calisa slowly, as if he wanted to torture her before he bit into her flesh. Then the fiendish creature tightened the circle and closed in for the kill.

I'm going to die. I hope it's quick. Resigned to her fate, Calisa watched as the shark started his final, death-dealing charge.

Calisa curled up in a ball, closed her eyes, and sucked in a deep breath, thinking it would be the last one she ever took. Floating in the calm water, she waited for the shark's razor-sharp teeth to rip into her trembling body. After several agonizing seconds, she heard a thud and a splash. But she was afraid to open her eyes. She didn't want the last picture in her mind to be the open mouth of a killer shark.

Then she heard beautiful sounds that gave her hope—dolphins clicking, whirring, and squealing. Calisa straightened up and stuck her head out of the water. She was stunned by what she saw.

Five yards (4.6 m) away from her, two adult dolphins were taking turns slamming into the side of the shark. With each blow, the shark thrashed in the water and backed away. When he tried to swim toward Calisa, the dolphins darted in front of him and wouldn't let him pass.

Moments later, two more dolphins appeared and rammed into the shark. He tried to bite them, but they were much too quick. Meanwhile, the little dolphin that had given Calisa a ride swam in a tight, protective circle around her.

By now, the battered shark had endured enough head butting from the dolphins. He turned and swam away.

Calisa bobbed in the water, overwhelmed by the drama that had unfolded in front of her. When she realized that the dolphins had saved her from a horrible death, she sobbed with relief.

The little dolphin hovered close to her, clicking and spewing water through his blow hole. "Oh, thank you," Calisa said, stroking his back. "Now I see what you were trying to do earlier. You knew there was a hungry shark between me and the boat, and you were trying to get me away from him. When I let go and started swimming toward the boat, you knew I wouldn't make it back without getting attacked, so you went and got help, didn't you? You dolphins really are the angels of the sea!"

CINDER THE SAVIOR

"Jerry! Wake up! Frankie is missing!"

Jerry Honeycutt bolted up from a sound sleep. His red-eyed wife, Krista, stood over him, weeping over the disappearance of their four-year-old son.

"Are you sure he's not hiding from you as a joke?" Jerry asked. "He knows he's not supposed to do anything but watch cartoons until we get up."

"I've looked everywhere in the house and outside. He's gone. And so is Cinder." Cinder was a black Labrador the Honeycutts had owned since they were newlyweds.

As Jerry hurriedly put on his clothes, he said, "If Cinder is with Frankie, chances are good he hasn't been kidnapped. He must be somewhere in the neighborhood."

"But what if he took off into the woods? There's the swamp and . . . oh, I don't want to think about it. Cinder just has to protect Frankie from any danger."

For a wedding present, a friend had let Jerry and Krista have the pick of the litter when his black Lab gave birth. They chose a gentle female with a crooked tail and named her Cinder.

The dog had such a sweet nature, she instantly turned strangers into friends. People could tell she was delighted to see them because she sat with her tail wagging like an out-of-control windshield wiper and stared with big brown eyes that could melt the coldest heart.

A few years after they married, the Honeycutts bought a house in a new development that backed up to a forest preserve. About a quarter mile (.4 km) away was an eerie swamp teeming with wildlife. Occasionally, critters such as rabbits, raccoons, and groundhogs showed up in the couple's backyard. Being nature lovers, they didn't mind—and neither did Cinder. Although she was just being curious when she approached them, the animals always fled in fear. They didn't need to be scared. Cinder loved virtually all living things.

Cinder's compassion shone brightest when she became a mother. Shortly after the dog had her own litter, Jerry found a pair of abandoned baby raccoons behind a woodpile in their backyard. The babies, no more than four inches (10.1 cm) long, were cold and hungry. He brought them into the house, where Krista tried to feed them warm milk from an eyedropper. But they wouldn't take the nourishment.

Fearing the infants would die, Krista glanced over at Cinder nursing her five puppies. "Jerry, what if we let Cinder try to save these baby coons?"

"It's worth a try. They're close to death."

Krista placed the raccoons next to Cinder on her sleeping pad. The dog sniffed the two mewing babies, not sure what to think. Then she nudged them toward her belly. They latched onto her and began to nurse. Seeing Cinder's amazing motherly instincts at work, Krista began to cry.

For the next eight weeks, Cinder played mom to the baby raccoons as well as her own puppies. She cleaned the coons and nursed them back to health. If they wandered too far away, she went after them and carried them back. She treated them as if they were her own puppies.

When the coons were finally weaned, they left to live in the woods. But one of them, Bandit, would return at night and sit on the back porch until Krista or Jerry gave him a cookie and a bowl of water.

When Frankie was born, the couple wondered how Cinder would react to a new member of the family. As Krista cradled the baby in her arms, the dog sniffed the infant and immediately barked her approval.

The boy and the dog grew to love each other. As a toddler, Frankie would pull on Cinder's tail or yank her ear, but she never snapped at him. Instead, she would lower her head and gently knock him down, which Frankie thought was great fun.

When Frankie acted up, Krista often had to scold him. At such times, Cinder whined and yelped, torn between loyalty to her mistress and love for little Frankie.

That love, and Cinder's motherly instincts, would save Frankie's life.

One Saturday, Frankie woke up early to an animal's screech. Adventurous by nature, the curly-haired youngster decided to investigate. Frankie figured the noise was a fairy in distress. The night before, his babysitter had read him a story about forest fairies and wood nymphs.

When Frankie opened the back door and stepped outside, Cinder jumped up and trotted after him. In the yard, the barefoot boy in Scooby-Doo pajamas stood still, waiting for a repeat of the sound. After a minute, he heard a shriek and then a long twitter. It was the cry of an Eastern screech owl, a bird that nests in tree holes. But to Frankie it was the scream of a desperate fairy.

"Did you hear that, Cinder?" Frankie whispered. "Let's see if we can find the fairy and help her."

Cinder whined. Her instincts told her this was a

bad idea, but she followed Frankie into the woods as he looked for a fairy in peril. Unfortunately, the only one in peril was Frankie.

They entered a cypress forest where colorful mosslike plants called lichens covered the tree trunks. Spanish moss clung to branches, hanging so low it tickled Frankie's head.

When he heard the screech again, Frankie told Cinder, "I think the fairy is real close." Again the dog whined, but she protectively tailed her young companion. They hiked deeper into the woods until they came to the swamp.

In front of Frankie was a thick green carpet of plants that looked sturdy enough to walk on. He couldn't tell that the carpet was made of water lettuces—floating plants that can't support anything heavier than a bird.

Frankie took one step onto the water lettuce and plunged into the muddy water underneath, sinking to the gooey bottom. He struggled to keep his head above the surface, but he was stuck in the thick mud.

"Help me! Help me!" he cried.

Cinder put a paw on the water lettuce to test it. Seeing that it wouldn't support her, she lay on her belly at the edge of the swamp and stuck her neck out so Frankie could grab her collar.

After several tries, Frankie's fingers wrapped around the collar. Then Cinder dug her claws into the soft ground and backed up. Slowly, she dragged

Frankie out of the muck and onto firmer ground. Caked in wet mud from head to toe, Frankie hugged his Lab. "Thanks, Cinder. That was icky."

The little boy snapped several fronds off a huge fern to wipe some of the muck from his pajamas. "Let's go home." He glanced around but couldn't figure out which way to walk. The swamp looked the same in all directions.

"Let's try this way." Frankie headed toward some tall saw grass, so named because the edges of each blade are as sharp as the teeth of a saw. But before Frankie could step foot into the saw grass, Cinder growled and bit into his pajama leg.

"Hey, let go!" Frankie ordered.

But the dog wouldn't obey. She just yanked him away until the boy finally got the message. "Okay, maybe we'll try that way," he said, pointing to a grassy area that seemed safer.

Meanwhile, back home, Jerry and Krista had frantically searched the neighborhood, but no one had seen Frankie or Cinder. The Honeycutts called the police, who immediately launched a search of the woods behind the house.

Unfortunately, the little boy was totally lost and walking even farther into the forest.

"I'm getting hungry, Cinder." Frankie munched on a few berries and offered some to his dog, but she refused to eat them. Then he came across some mushrooms that had bright red caps. They looked like the ones his mother often prepared—sliced portabellos smothered with tomato sauce and served over toast.

Frankie assumed that the red mushrooms by his feet had tomato sauce on them. "Mmm, these look good." He picked one and was about to take a bite when he noticed Cinder staring at the mushroom.

"Here, Cinder, you can take the first bite. You must be hungry, too."

Cinder sniffed the mushroom—then jumped up and batted it out of Frankie's hand.

"Hey, that's not nice." Frankie picked up the mushroom and raised it to his mouth, but the dog knocked it from his grasp again. "Stop that!" Frankie scolded her. He plucked another red-capped mushroom. But instead of trying to eat it, he put it in the pocket of his pajama top. He figured he would snack on it later when Cinder wasn't quite so touchy.

"I don't hear the fairy anymore," Frankie said. "I hope she's all right." Then he began to pout. "I wish I was all right."

A half hour later, they came to a stream. "I don't like it here. I wish a fairy would come and take us home."

Cinder began to growl. "Don't you like fairies? I do." The Lab growled again.

Frankie shrugged and began walking alongside the creek. Suddenly, Cinder bounded in front of him and pushed him down.

"I don't want to play now." Frankie got up, but he took only a few steps before Cinder knocked him over again. "Stop it, Cinder. That's not funny." Frankie waved his finger in front of the dog's nose. "You're starting to make me . . ."

His voice trailed off when he noticed a snake slithering across a rock nearby. Its flat-topped head was wider than its neck, and black bands crossed its brown body. Frankie had never seen a snake like this before, but he could tell it wasn't friendly, especially after it opened its mouth, exposing a white lining. It was a poisonous cottonmouth—one of the deadliest, most aggressive snakes in the South—and it was on the attack.

Frankie froze, but Cinder didn't. She pounced on the snake, which reared its head and struck at the dog. Cinder dodged it and lunged again, trying to bite the snake from behind. The cottonmouth was just as quick. It snapped its head back, jabbing at the dog's face, but missed.

Cinder leaped on the snake's back near its head and chomped down hard. The snake hissed. In a last act of defiance, it sank its fangs into the Lab's left front paw. After the cottonmouth had injected its poison into the dog, the snake died.

Cinder let out a high-pitched yelp and backed off. She hobbled over to Frankie, who was still on the ground, too shaken to move. The dog lay down and began licking her wounded paw, whining pitifully.

Frankie began to cry. He knew they were lost, and he was afraid they would never get home. He wondered what other terrors lurked in the swamp.

As he wept, the little boy buried his head in Cinder's side. Cinder whimpered, partly from the pain of the snake bite and partly because she sensed Frankie's fear. She took turns licking her wounded paw and Frankie's hand.

Minutes later, the Lab's ears perked up. She sniffed the air and tried to get up. Seeing the dog stir, Frankie stopped crying and rubbed his wet face with his dirty pajama sleeve. "Another mean animal?" Frankie asked uneasily.

Cinder barked, waited a few seconds, then barked again. Her tail began wagging. Frankie knew something was out there and feared the worst. He climbed a small sycamore tree, hoping to hide from whatever was heading their way.

Meanwhile, Cinder limped away from the creek, all the while barking furiously. "Stay with me, Cinder. Please!" Frankie whispered. "No, don't go!"

Holding her injured paw off the ground, Cinder hopped into the tall grass. She soon came face-to-face with a bloodhound leading a squad of searchers.

"That's their dog!" shouted one of the officers. He kneeled down next to Cinder and gently rubbed her face. "Hi, girl. Where's Frankie? Can you take us to Frankie?"

The black Lab barked, turned around, and limped

back toward the sycamore tree where Frankie was still perched.

"Frankie? Frankie? Where are you?" the rescuers called.

"In the tree!" the little boy shouted. He climbed down and ran into the arms of the officer. "We got lost and I was scared and I want my mommy and daddy," Frankie bawled.

"You're safe, son. We're going to take you home now."

Frankie was hoisted onto the officer's back for the one-mile (1.6-km) trek to the house. The search team was deep in the tall grass when Frankie cried out, "Where's Cinder? Cinder! Come on, girl!"

But Cinder didn't come. She was sprawled on the ground, panting heavily. Frankie leaped off the officer's back and ran to his dog. "Cinder!"

"What's wrong with her?" asked the officer.

"She got in a fight with that snake over there," Frankie replied.

A searcher looked at the dead reptile and said, "It's a cottonmouth."

"The bite could be fatal," the officer said. "There's a clearing a few hundred yards from here. Call in the chopper. We'll airlift the boy and his dog. Have a vet waiting at the command center. Tell him the dog needs immediate treatment for a cottonmouth bite."

The helicopter soon whisked Frankie and Cinder to the command center, where Jerry and Krista had a tearful reunion with their scratched and mud-caked son. Meanwhile, the vet rushed Cinder to the animal clinic for emergency treatment.

Back home, Frankie told his parents how Cinder had pulled him out of the muck and fought the snake. As he stripped off his filthy pajamas, the red-capped mushroom he had saved fell out of his pocket.

"What's this?" Krista asked.

"I picked it because it looks just like the 'shrooms you make. I was hungry and I wanted to eat it, but Cinder kept knocking it out of my hand."

Krista slapped her hand over her mouth to keep from bursting into tears. She turned to Jerry and exclaimed, "Cinder knew that this mushroom is poisonous! If Frankie had eaten it . . ." She couldn't finish.

"That dog amazes me more each day," marveled Jerry. "She just has to pull through."

The next three hours seemed to take forever while the family worried about the dog's fate. Then came the call from the vet. "Mrs. Honeycutt, good news. Cinder is going to make it. The antivenin serum is working."

Krista screamed with happiness. "Yes! Yes! Yes!"

"She's one tough dog," the doctor added.

"Yes," agreed Krista, "but she has the softest heart in the world."

CAT'S INCREDIBLE!

Shannon O'Leary knew Sparky was special from the moment he was born.

The kitten entered the world with six paws—two on each front leg and one on each hind leg. The extra paws spread out to the side when he stood, but they were hard to notice when he walked. The kitty had at least the nub of ten toes on each front paw.

"A kitten with an extra toe on each paw will happen maybe one time in a thousand," the veterinarian told Shannon. "But I've never seen a kitten with extra paws. I'd say he's one in a million."

Shannon didn't know until years later just how right the vet was.

Because of his extra claws in front, the brown-white-and-black calico climbed trees better than the rest of the litter could. He loved to harass the squirrels in the O'Learys' yard. They had always felt safe in the trees—until Sparky joined Shannon's family. The squirrels had to leap from tree to tree to escape his unwanted attention.

Sparky became so good at climbing that he once scaled a telephone pole—and caused all sorts of commotion.

As Sparky lazily watched the traffic below him, an elderly woman spotted him. Assuming the cat could not get down, she called the phone company and pleaded for someone to rescue the animal. A lineman arrived an hour later and began going up the pole. Scared by the sight of a stranger wearing a hard hat, Sparky meowed and hissed. Below, a crowd had gathered to watch the rescue.

When the lineman reached the top, Sparky became even more frightened. He walked out onto one of the crossbeams of the telephone pole, then leaped like a squirrel onto the branch of a nearby tree. The branch snapped under his weight but didn't break off completely.

Sparky's double front paws wrapped around the branch, his hind legs kicking out in panic. Suddenly, the branch split, and he tumbled onto a lower, thicker limb. Once again, he used his front paws to stop his fall. The limb held, and Sparky scrambled to the tree trunk and scooted down to the ground.

The onlookers, who had gathered at the base of the telephone pole, cheered. Whether out of embarrassment or shyness, Sparky streaked behind the house. Nobody saw him until early evening—sitting on the peak of the O'Learys' garage.

Sparky had been a present for Shannon's tenth birthday. Her older sister, Kate, already had a pet, Lacy Jane—a pampered brown toy poodle who had her toenails painted bright red and wore white ribbons in her hair. At first, the dog wouldn't have much to do with the kitten and growled whenever he came too close. But eventually she grew to accept the feline. The only time they squabbled was when Sparky tried to nibble at the food in Lacy Jane's dish. She would yip at him until he stormed off—but not before he spat at her and took a swipe at her nose.

On nice days, Sparky and Lacy Jane napped in the backyard. The poodle liked to snooze under a shade tree while Sparky's favorite spot was on the roof of the back porch. He would climb a trellis to the roof and sun himself. Whenever the mood struck him, the cat would jump down, slip through the ficus hedge, and tour the neighborhood.

Sparky knew where every dog in the neighborhood lived. If a dog was tied up, Sparky tormented him by prancing just out of reach, ignoring the snarling and barking. But he steered clear of the free-roaming dogs. Occasionally, he was chased and needed to run up a tree to escape the deadly jaws of his canine pursuer. Other times, he squirmed through the hedge and into the safety of his own yard.

Lacy Jane caused dogs to bark wildly too. One day, Kate walked her poodle past the Hendersons' house. A pit bull named Crusher slammed against the chainlink fence, growling and snarling at the prissy pooch. He went nuts every time he saw Lacy Jane.

"Oh, shut up, Crusher," yelled Kate. "I'm getting tired of all your carrying on."

Just then, Kirby Henderson, Crusher's fifteen-year-old owner, stepped from behind the house. "Don't talk to my dog that way," he snapped.

"Your dog is a nuisance, Kirby," claimed Kate. "He's always barking."

"He only barks at people he doesn't like."

"Like everyone."

"At least Crusher is a real dog, not like that sissy poodle of yours."

"Lacy Jane is a smart, loving dog."

"Yeah, right. She's good for nothing. She wouldn't even make an afternoon snack for Crusher."

"Just keep that brute locked up."

Kirby went over to the gate and rested his hand on the latch. "Hey, Kate, all I have to do is move my fingers just a little bit and the gate will swing open and—"

"Don't you dare!"

Shuddering at the thought, Kate scooped up Lacy Jane and hurried on, glancing over her shoulder as Kirby laughed ghoulishly.

"Tell that sister of yours to keep her cat out of my

yard," he shouted at Kate. "If he messes with Crusher one more time, I'm going to let my dog out so he can chase that cat—and eat him!" Kirby laughed again.

That night at the dinner table, Kate told the family about the incident. "I'm afraid of that dog," she said. "If Crusher gets free, he could hurt someone. There are little kids all over this neighborhood."

"The problem is that Kirby isn't a very good pet owner," said her father. "Pit bulls aren't mean and bloodthirsty at birth. They're taught to be vicious by their owners. Crusher is learning from Kirby."

"Kirby is a creepazoid," Kate declared. "He's always in the principal's office."

"I wish Sparky would stay away from that place," said Shannon. "I worry that someday Kirby *will* sic Crusher on him."

"Sparky will be fine," Kate assured her. "He'll just run up a tree."

"Yeah," countered Shannon, "but Crusher is so big and mean he's liable to chop down the tree with his teeth."

Kate avoided walking by Kirby Henderson's house for several weeks. But one evening, she made plans to go over to her friend Jillian's house so they could work on a social studies project together. Jillian, who asked Kate to bring Lacy Jane with her, lived four doors away from the Hendersons.

Kate was hoping that Crusher wouldn't notice Lacy Jane as she walked by the house. But he did—and he let everyone else on the block know it too. Snarling and barking, the pit bull followed Kate and Lacy Jane along the fence. Then he slammed against the gate. It sprang open—and he charged after his prey.

Kate screamed, picked up Lacy Jane, and began running. But she didn't see that a tree root had lifted up a slab of the sidewalk. She tripped on the crack and tumbled to the ground, tossing Lacy Jane onto the grass so she wouldn't fall on her dog.

As Crusher bore down on them, Kate braced herself for the attack. But when he was about ten feet (3 m) away, Crusher jerked to a stop so violently, he almost did a backflip. To Kate's great relief, he had run out of chain.

While Crusher yelped, Kate heard Kirby's unmistakable laugh. "Good thing Crusher had only fifty feet (15 m) of chain. Another ten feet (3 m) and you would've been his dinner."

"Kirby, you creep, you opened the gate on purpose!"

"Maybe I did, maybe he did. He's one clever dog."

"He's one *mean* dog."

Through it all, Crusher continued woofing and growling. Kate picked up Lacy Jane and hurried over to Jillian's house.

One afternoon a week later, Lacy Jane was gnawing on an old bone in the backyard. She yipped at Sparky when he came over to see if the bone was something he wanted to eat. Sparky spat at the poodle and then trotted off to snooze on the flat roof of the back porch. He scaled the trellis and walked along the edge of the roof, soaking up the heat radiating off the shingles. He yawned and stretched out for a long nap.

Soon Lacy Jane heard the girls come home from school. She left her bone and began waddling toward the back porch to greet her mistress.

"Hi, Lacy Jane!" shouted Kate.

The poodle wagged her tail and broke into a trot, then suddenly she froze in her tracks. Crashing through the ficus hedge was Crusher—and he zeroed in on Lacy Jane.

Kate screamed, "Lacy Jane! Run!" while Shannon looked on in horror.

The pit bull had somehow escaped from his yard and now was ready to pounce on the helpless poodle. Lacy Jane made a mad dash for safety, but she wasn't fast enough. Within seconds, Crusher body-slammed the dog to the ground.

The savage pit bull began mauling the yelping, squealing poodle. He pinned her to the ground and tore at her chest and throat.

"Get away! Get away!" Kate shrieked. She grabbed Shannon's arm and pleaded, "Do something!"

Shannon rushed inside for a broom, while Kate ran to the side of the house to fetch the hose.

Startled awake by the noise of the attack and the girls' screams, Sparky gave an angry hiss and flew into action. He ran to the edge of the roof and then made an incredible flying leap—right onto Crusher's head.

At first, the pit bull paid no attention. He was too involved in mangling his prey. But within seconds, Crusher stopped biting Lacy Jane as he realized he was the one being attacked.

Sparky sank all six of his clawed paws into the dog's head and raked the double front paws across the sides of Crusher's face. The dog tried to shake off his foe, but Sparky simply dug his claws deeper into the dog's skin.

Crusher bucked like a bronco, but the brave cat held on with the skill of a professional rodeo rider. Sparky's razor-sharp teeth tore at the dog's ears.

Howling, the bewildered and hurt pit bull rolled on his side and used his powerful front paws to knock Sparky off his head. But before Crusher could get up, the cat leaped on the dog's back, driving his sharp claws into Crusher's fur.

The dog ran around in circles, shaking as hard as he could. Finally, he threw off the cat, who landed hard in Lacy Jane's water bowl. The pit bull, bleeding from his face and back, ran toward the hedge, turning back just once to make sure the ferocious cat wasn't chasing him. Sparky started to pursue the dog, but thought better of it. Instead, the cat scampered over to Lacy Jane, who was lying on her side, bleeding badly from gashes in her neck, throat, and chest.

"Lacy Jane!" Kate wailed. "Don't die!" While Kate ran into the house to grab a towel, Shannon tried to comfort the dog by stroking her head. With her other hand, Shannon gently picked up her cat.

"Oh, Sparky, are you hurt?" A quick exam revealed no bites or cuts. "What a brave little cat you are."

By now Kate had returned with a towel and was wiping her poodle's deep wounds. "We've got to get her to the vet's. Maybe Mrs. Nelson can take us. We don't have time to get Mom out of work."

Just then Kirby stuck his head over the hedge. "Hi. I'm looking for Crusher. He got out and I've been . . ." He stopped when he saw the fury in the girls' eyes and the limp, bleeding poodle in Kate's arms. "What happened to your dog?"

"Crusher attacked Lacy Jane!" Kate snarled.

Kirby looked down at his side. "Crusher, there you are! Hey, what happened to you? Your face is all cut up."

"Sparky did it," boasted Shannon. "And I'm glad he did. He saved Lacy Jane's life."

"Are you telling me that stupid cat of yours beat up my pit bull?"

"Yeah, I am."

Kirby shook his head and walked off, muttering to Crusher, "How could you let a cat whip you like that?"

Lacy Jane was rushed to the animal clinic, where her wounds were cleaned and stitched. "She's very lucky," the vet told the girls. "She'll survive. If that cat hadn't run off the pit bull, Lacy Jane definitely would've been killed. It's just amazing that such a small cat could be fierce enough to beat up a big, vicious dog."

Authorities fined the Hendersons, who agreed to pay the poodle's medical bills and give Crusher away.

As for Lacy Jane, she recovered from her serious injuries, but she never went anywhere near the Hendersons' yard, even though Crusher was gone for good. There was one other thing Lacy Jane never did after the attack: She no longer complained if Sparky snatched a bite of her food.

GATOR BAIT

"No, get away from me! Aaahhh!"

The shrill cry of a panic-stricken woman jolted Luis and Isabella Gomez as they ate lunch in their kitchen.

"Luis, did you hear that?" asked the elderly woman, dropping her sandwich on her plate. "It sounds like it's coming from next door."

Luis set down his drink and opened the window that faced the home of Eduardo and Corazon Fernandez. But he couldn't see anything through the six-foot-high (2-m) hibiscus hedge between his house and theirs.

"Get away!" wailed the female voice. "Get away!"

"*Por Dios!* That sounds like Corazon Fernandez," the alarmed Isabella exclaimed.

"How can you tell? We've only met our neighbors once since we moved in last week."

"If it's not her, then it's her daughter. Someone is in trouble! Do something, Luis, *ahora mismo!*"

Luis hustled out the back door and peeked through the hedge at his neighbor's pool and patio. His suspicions were aroused when he saw that the Fernandezes' sliding glass door and screen were open—not a common sight in south Florida during the summer because of the heat and bugs.

Another shriek. "No! No! No!"

There was no doubt that the frantic person was inside the Fernandezes' house. Luis ran to his kitchen and called 911. "This is Luis Gomez at 124 Orchid Lane. A woman is screaming at the Fernandez house next door. I think an intruder has broken in and is attacking her. Please hurry!"

Within minutes, two squad cars pulled up to the house. Four policemen, crouched low with their guns drawn, crept around to the patio in the back.

"Get away from me! Aaahhh!"

Hearing the cry, the officers charged through the open sliding door, shouting, "Police! Don't anybody move!"

To their befuddlement they failed to find anyone home. The only sign of life was a parrot in a cage in the corner of the living room. The policemen, however, were convinced they had found a crime scene because the living room looked ransacked.

Cushions from the couch and chairs were scattered on the floor. The coffee table lay on its side, and clothes were strewn everywhere.

"Seems like a struggle took place here, Sarge," noted one of the officers. As the police returned to the pool area, a girl and a boy dashed around the corner and smacked into them.

"Halt!" ordered the sergeant. "Who are you?"

"I'm Anna-Maria Fernandez and this is my brother, Raul," answered the startled twelve-year-old girl.

"Who else is home?"

"No one. Mama is at the grocery store. Why?"

"We had a report of a woman screaming in your house."

A screech from the living room shattered the air. "No! No! Get away from me!"

The police spun on their heels, drew their guns, and rushed back into the house.

"No!" shouted Anna-Maria. "That's Rita!"

Inside, the police were perplexed because they still couldn't find a screaming woman. "Rita! Rita! Where are you?" shouted the sergeant.

Anna-Maria followed them inside, swallowed hard, and said, "Don't get mad, but Rita isn't a woman. She's an African grey." Then she pointed to the parrot—a pigeon-sized, light gray bird sporting a bright red tail.

"Police! Squawk! Police," the parrot jabbered.

"You mean that bird has been doing all the

screaming?" asked the dumbfounded sergeant.

"Rita imitates voices and things," Anna-Maria hesitantly explained. "She says lots of stuff from TV."

Pointing to the mess in the room, the sergeant asked, "What about all this and the open door?"

Ten-year-old Raul gulped. In a barely audible voice, he said, "I was making a fort with the cushions. I ambushed Anna-Maria when she came into the room with the laundry and chased her outside. I forgot to close the door. We were just playing around."

The sergeant shook his head in disbelief. He walked to the caged bird and grunted, "So you're the one causing all this fuss, huh?"

In a gruff man's voice, Rita snarled, "I ain't talkin'!"

The truth was, nothing could shut Rita up. She engaged in constant chatter. It was a good thing the parrot did, because that chatter helped save Anna-Maria's life.

Rita was born in Ghana, Africa, and was exported to the United States. The Fernandez family bought her in a pet shop when she was six months old.

Like many African greys, Rita had a natural ability to mimic sounds she heard around the house—creaking doors, running water, coughs, telephone rings, even kissing. She could imitate the voice of any member of the family and knew more than two hundred words in English and Spanish.

The kids painfully learned to be careful about what they said in front of her.

One day, Anna-Maria mentioned to her girlfriend Geena how much she liked their classmate Jorge. Rita filed this comment away for future use. About two weeks later, Jorge stopped by the house. Anna-Maria opened the door and said, "Oh, hi, Jorge!" A moment later, Rita, imitating Anna-Maria's voice, announced, "Jorge is the coolest guy in class. I think he's so cute!" Anna-Maria turned beet-red from embarrassment.

Raul had his own mortifying moment. His mother often scolded him for belching after he drank from a can of soda—a bad habit that Rita duly noted. One afternoon, the priest from their parish visited them. When Rita saw Raul bring the priest a can of soda, she immediately made the sound of the can being opened, followed by glugging noises and a loud burp.

The parrot lived in two cages—one in the living room and the other on the patio by the pool so she could watch the wild birds. Her cages were placed in spots where the Fernandezes spent the most time. That way, Rita was made to feel like an important part of the family.

The Fernandezes gave Rita attention even on busy days. They stopped by her cage to say hello or they whistled from another room just to let her know that she hadn't been forgotten. When the family was gone for the day, they often turned on the TV to keep her company. Unfortunately, the day before her screaming brought the police, Rita had been watching an intense police drama.

The Fernandezes were avid fans of the University of Florida Gators football team and watched all its games on TV. Naturally, Rita learned to yell "Touchdown!" and "Go, Gators!" Whenever she saw the Florida mascot—a student dressed in a blue and orange alligator costume—she would bellow, "Gator . . . grrr . . . gator!"

The family proudly showed off Rita's gator growl to other fans. But one day, when they asked her to perform it, she chanted, "Goooooo, Dawgs! Sic 'em! Woof! Woof! Woof!" The family was appalled. She had learned the cheer of the Gators' arch rival—the University of Georgia Bulldogs, whom the Florida team had played the week before.

One night, the family had gone to bed when they heard Rita twitter, "Gator! Gator!" Anna-Maria walked downstairs and told the parrot, "*Silencio*, Rita. Football season doesn't start for months. Now go to sleep."

The next morning, Anna-Maria went out to the pool for a swim. She discovered one of the inflatable rafts lying torn by the bushes next to the deck. "Raul, did you do this?"

"No," her brother answered. "Why do you always blame me when something breaks?"

"You're always the most likely suspect."

"I used it last, but I didn't tear it or leave it in the

bushes like that. A raccoon must have done it. Or maybe it was the Gallegas' dog. He's always snooping around here."

The next night, the family was watching the news on television. The sports segment featured a clip of a Florida football game from the previous season. When a shot of the mascot appeared, Rita snarled, "Gator . . . grrr . . . gator!" The family cheered.

Later, as they headed to their bedrooms, she gave them her usual send-off: "Night, night! Squawk. Night, night."

About two in the morning, Anna-Maria awoke to Rita's loud growling. "Gator . . . grrrr . . . gator." Anna-Maria was too tired to go downstairs to quiet the bird. Her sleeping parents and brother didn't even hear the parrot.

Rather than keep quiet, Rita growled louder. "Gator . . . grrr . . . gator." Then in an announcer's voice, she added, "See how those teeth shine!"

Anna-Maria sat up in bed, trying to figure out why Rita was behaving this way in the middle of the night. Then she heard Rita's shrill voice scream, "Gator . . . uh-oh . . . gator!"

Annoyed that the parrot had disrupted her sleep, Anna-Maria marched down to the living room. "Am I going to have to put the cover over your cage? Now shut up, will you?"

Anna-Maria noticed that Rita was picking her feathers. Several feathers lay at the bottom of the cage.

The girl knew this was a sign of emotional stress in birds. She took the parrot out of the cage and let Rita climb up her arm and onto her shoulder.

"What's wrong, Rita?"

The parrot flapped her wings and hopped from one foot to the other, chattering, "Gator bait! Squawk! Gator bait!"

"What are you talking about?" As Anna-Maria put Rita back into the cage, she gasped in horror. Her eyes focused on the toothy grin of an eight-foot-long (2.4-m) alligator whose snout was pressing against the sliding door. The gator had come from the canal behind their house.

"Oh, no, *increíble!*" she murmured to Rita. "That's why you were making such a racket about gators! You were trying to warn us. Good, Rita, good."

"Rita good! Squawk. Rita good!"

"The gator must have been here last night, too, because you were making noise then, and we found the raft torn up."

Anna-Maria was scared but also fascinated. She knew she should wake up her parents, but she couldn't tear herself away just yet. Figuring she was perfectly safe behind the door, she moved closer for a better look at the animal. She aimed a lamp at the gator and gasped again. Raul had forgotten to close the sliding glass door. All that stood between her and the alligator was the flimsy screen door.

Just as Anna-Maria realized the danger she was in,

the gator crashed through the screen and marched into the house. Panic-stricken, Anna-Maria leaped back and fell over a chair.

The gator, now only five feet (1.5 m) away from the girl, opened its mouth and hissed. As it crawled toward her, Anna-Maria let out a bloodcurdling scream.

Meanwhile, Rita fluttered to the floor. Although she couldn't fly because her wings had been clipped, she bravely harassed the gator. Standing at the opposite side of the room from where Anna-Maria lay, she hissed and growled, causing the gator to turn its attention toward her.

Seconds later, Eduardo bounded down the stairs. "Daddy!" Anna-Maria cried out to him. "There's a gator in the house! Help!"

"Gator bait!" Rita screeched. "Gator bait!"

While Rita distracted the gator, Anna-Maria picked up the chair and threw it at the huge reptile. Eduardo grabbed his daughter by the arm and yanked her away. Then he raced upstairs, pulled out a .357 Magnum from a chest of drawers, loaded it, and sprinted down the steps again.

Its mouth open, the growling gator headed for Rita, who was still hopping on the floor, squawking and hissing at the menacing animal. Just as the gator was about to chomp Rita, Eduardo fired three shots into the reptile's head. The animal fell dead in its tracks, its jaws snapping shut just inches from the bird.

"Right between the eyes!" squawked Rita. "Right between the eyes!"

Eduardo warily walked over to the gator and confirmed it was dead. Then he picked up the trembling parrot. "You are a very brave bird, Rita!" he said.

Anna-Maria gave the parrot a big kiss. "You saved my life by distracting that gator! You're the best!"

"Rita the best! Squawk! Rita the best."

The reptile's break-in had no lasting effects on the parrot—except for one thing. She no longer liked to watch the Florida Gators.

THE DYNAMIC DUO

Bo Whitney had two dogs—Ziggy the Border collie and Freda the Rottweiler.

Ziggy was an extremely smart, energetic black-and-white dog. If you asked him for a soda, he'd nudge open the cooler, pick up a can in his mouth, and bring it to you. If you made a gunfire noise, he'd play dead. Ziggy could even snare a tossed Frisbee every time. In fact, he was the top canine Frisbee catcher at the Pecatonica County Fair for three straight years.

Freda, in contrast, was a one-hundred-pound (45-kg) lump, a sweet giant whose favorite pastime was sleeping on the back deck. Once, she'd even slept through an outdoor rock concert. She appeared fearsome and dangerous, but anyone who looked at her wrinkled gray-black face saw the big brown eyes of a gentle soul.

Bo admitted that Ziggy was his favorite. But the thirteen-year-old boy had a special fondness for Freda. If it hadn't been for her strength—and Ziggy's quick thinking—Bo would have drowned.

Bo and his family lived in a sprawling ranch house on land that butted up against a lake fed by a rushing trout stream. Bo, his brother, and two sisters had all sorts of pets—two cats, a ferret, three rabbits, and a raccoon. Freda joined the family when Bo was six. Ziggy arrived two years later.

At first, Freda wasn't too thrilled with the new addition. She growled and snarled, trying to intimidate the much smaller dog. In the rare moments that Freda showed any energy, she chased him. But Ziggy could dodge and dart and run circles around the big canine oaf. When Freda realized Ziggy enjoyed being chased, she quit doing it.

About four months after joining the Whitneys' household, Ziggy finally won Freda over. The family was planning a cookout, and several frozen steaks were thawing in a cooler on the deck. Using his paws and nose, Ziggy opened the unlatched lid. He snatched two steaks and scampered under a nearby hammock where Freda was napping.

Rather than being a hog, Ziggy shared his booty. He and Freda were pals from then on, although Freda still got irritated when Ziggy wanted to play and she wanted to sleep.

As the youngest in the family, Bo spent the most

time with Ziggy. It was obvious that the Border collie favored him over the other Whitneys—especially after Bo discovered Ziggy's amazing talent for catching a Frisbee.

"You play Frisbee with him, you make his day," Bo explained to his parents. "That's what he lives for—to play Frisbee." The two practiced for thirty minutes a day after school and developed a routine that earned them trophies at the county fair. For one throw, Ziggy made a 360-degree twirl before snaring the flying disk in his mouth. He jumped on Bo's back and vaulted into the air to catch another Frisbee. It was nothing for him to grasp a sailing Frisbee from forty yards (36.4 m) away. As Bo and Ziggy practiced their Frisbee act, Freda was content to watch them from the deck.

When Bo wasn't playing with Ziggy, he spent the rest of his free time fishing in the lake. One cold, blustery Saturday, he bundled up in a heavy wool sweater, a thick jacket, and trail boots and went down to the lake to catch trout. Ziggy followed him while Freda, as usual, snored on the deck.

"Ziggy, I don't want you sticking your nose in my tackle box," Bo warned after they stepped onto the dock. "And stay away from my catches." Ziggy had a tendency to leap on any flopping fish that Bo had landed on the dock. "The last time you almost got yourself hooked. So stay back." Ziggy's ears drooped as though he understood every word Bo said.

"After I reel in a few trout, we'll play Frisbee,

okay?" As soon as he heard the word "Frisbee," Ziggy jumped and barked. "Not now, Ziggy, but soon. Let me catch dinner first."

About twenty minutes later, Bo announced, "Hey, I've got a bite! Feels like a keeper!" He netted a fat trout and laid it on the dock. Squatting on his heels like a baseball catcher, Bo turned away to get a pair of needle-nose pliers out of his tackle box so he could pull out the hook. As Bo reached into the box, an osprey—a large, hawklike bird—swooped down and tried to swipe the fish.

Ziggy growled, causing the osprey to back off at the last second. Letting out a piercing cry, the bird hovered low over the dock. This annoyed Ziggy so much, he tried to bite the osprey.

As he had practiced so many times with the Frisbee, Ziggy raced up Bo's back, leaped into the air, and tried to catch the bird. But the osprey zoomed off, and the dog bellyflopped into the water.

Bo was not expecting Ziggy to run up his back. Because the teen was squatting, the dog's impact caused the boy to lose his balance. Bo pitched forward and hit his head on a cleat, a piece of metal on the dock. Dazed and hurt, he tumbled into the frigid lake, where the water was over ten feet (3 m) deep.

Unfortunately, Bo had never learned to swim. Semiconscious, he began to sink as his heavy clothes filled up with water. *What's happening?* Bo thought fuzzily. *Why am I in the water? Which way is up?*

Meanwhile, Ziggy swam to shore and jumped onto the dock, looking for Bo. When he reached the end of the dock and saw Bo thrashing under the water, Ziggy dived back into the lake to save his master.

The cold water helped clear the fuzziness from Bo's head. But once he realized where he was, he panicked. As he struggled to the surface, his heavy, waterlogged clothes made him feel as if he were wearing a lead suit and concrete boots.

Bo's feet hit the bottom of the lake. He kicked hard, pushing himself up through the water. He surfaced just long enough to suck in a quick breath of air. "Help! Help!" he shouted. But he knew it was useless to yell. None of his family was home.

As Bo struggled in the water, Ziggy dog-paddled out to him. "Ziggy!" Bo cried between coughs. "Help me, boy! Help me!" When his loyal pet reached him, Bo threw his arms around him. But they both sank because Bo and his heavy clothes weighed so much. The dog, in danger of drowning, instinctively squirmed free.

No, don't leave me! Ziggy, help me! I'm drowning! Bo thought as he slipped deeper under the water. His burning lungs ready to burst, Bo felt his feet touch the bottom again. He pushed off and broke the surface, gagging and sputtering for breath. "Ziggy! Where are you? Help me!"

Bo's panicked splashing had moved him farther out into the lake. He began to feel his strength seeping away. *I've got to get out of these clothes. They're dragging me down.*

Taking a deep breath, he dipped below the surface and tried to lighten his load. However, his motions were slow and sluggish. He slipped out of his jacket but was too weak to take off his sweater or untie his boots.

Bo clawed his way to the surface for another gulp of precious air. Before he went under again, his eyes searched the bank in hopes that maybe, by a stroke of good fortune, someone had heard his cries. He saw no one, not even Ziggy, but he could hear the dog barking furiously.

Moments before, Ziggy had scrambled to the bank and streaked toward the house. Hearing his frenzied barking, Freda, who had been sleeping on the back deck, sat up. When Ziggy reached her, he continued to yelp, then headed back toward the lake.

Freda joined Ziggy, and they sprinted to the end of the dock. About forty feet (12 m) away, Bo was flailing under the water, his head popping up every few seconds. He was surviving by sheer willpower and his ability to push off from the bottom so that he could surface briefly for air. But he was rapidly becoming fatigued. *I don't know if I can make it. I'm so tired. How can I get back to shore?*

Seeing Bo in serious trouble, Freda jumped into the lake and paddled straight to the drowning boy. "Freda! Help me!" gasped Bo as he grabbed her. But, just as it had with Ziggy, Bo's weight dragged Freda under. She broke free from his grasp and swam to the surface. *Don't go! Stay, Freda! Please!*

Freda didn't leave him. She paddled near his submerged head. This time, rather than put all his weight on her back, Bo clutched Freda's right hind leg and held on. Barely able to keep her head above water, the Rottweiler gradually towed Bo toward shore.

When they reached shallow water, Bo let go. He staggered up the bank, crumpled in a heap, and passed out. A few minutes later, he regained consciousness. Both dogs were licking his face and whining for him to get up. "Ziggy, Freda," he mumbled. "Boy, do I love you guys."

Ziggy and Freda presented him with a chorus of happy barks. His throat sore and his lungs aching, Bo sat up and hugged his two dogs. When he felt strong enough, the weary teen stood up and tottered toward the house. Seeing her master's wobbly walk, Freda stayed by his side so he could steady himself by placing his hand on her back.

Once he got inside, Bo stripped off his wet clothes, dried his chilled body, and wrapped up in a cozy bathrobe. Then he toweled off the dogs. He built a roaring blaze in the fireplace and ordered them to sit by the warm hearth. At first, they were wary because they weren't usually allowed in this part of the house. But this was a special occasion.

After taking a hot shower and putting on dry clothes, Bo was still shaking from his near-drowning.

As he entered the family room, he found his mother with her hands on her hips. "Why are the dogs in here?"

"They deserve it, Mom. They saved my life."

Bo recounted his harrowing ordeal. When he finished, Bo scratched Ziggy's chin and didn't say a word for a minute. Then he blurted, "Ziggy knew he wasn't strong enough to save me because he weighs only twenty-five pounds (11 kg). So he ran to get Freda, who's four times as big and strong as a horse. Ziggy brought her to the lake to rescue me."

Bo dropped to his knees between the two canines and rubbed their heads. "These are two super dogs. Ziggy and I might be a great Frisbee team, but as lifesavers, nobody can beat the team of Ziggy and Freda."